CW01262290

Disney · PIXAR
TOY STORY
5-MINUTE STORIES

SCHOLASTIC
SYDNEY   AUCKLAND   NEW YORK   TORONTO   LONDON   MEXICO CITY
NEW DELHI   HONG KONG   BUENOS AIRES   PUERTO RICO

TABLE OF CONTENTS

A New Toy 9

Moving Day 27

Woody's Big Adventure 45

A Wild Ride 63

Toys That Go Bump in the Night 81

Rocket Launchers 99

Woody's Quest for a Date 117

Toys in Paradise 135

So Long, Partner 145

All stories based on the characters from the movies *Toy Story* Copyright © 1995 Disney Enterprises, Inc., *Toy Story 2* Copyright © 1999 Disney/Pixar, Original *Toy Story* elements © Disney Enterprises, Inc., and *Toy Story 3* Copyright © 2010 Disney/Pixar. Slinky® Dog is a registered trademark of Poof-Slinky, Inc. © Poof-Slinky, Inc. Playskool Portable Baby Monitor® is a registered trademark of Hasbro, Inc. Used with permission. © Hasbro, Inc. All rights reserved. Pez® is a registered trademark of Pez Candy, Inc. Used with permission. All rights reserved. Mr. and Mrs. Potato Head® are registered trademarks of Hasbro, Inc. Used with permission. © Hasbro, Inc. All rights reserved. Playskool Rockin' Robot Mr. Mike® is a registered trademark of Hasbro, Inc. Used with permission. © Hasbro, Inc. All rights reserved. Tinkertoys® is a registered trademark of Hasbro, Inc. Used with permission. © Hasbro, Inc. All rights reserved. Monopoly® is a registered trademark of Hasbro, Inc. Used with permission. © Hasbro, Inc. All rights reserved.

'A New Toy' written by Kate Egan. Copyright © 2019 Disney Enterprises, Inc.

'Moving Day' written by Kate Egan. Copyright © 2019 Disney Enterprises, Inc.

'Woody's Big Adventure' written by Annie Auerbach. Copyright © 2019 Disney Enterprises, Inc./Pixar

'A Wild Ride' written by Annie Auerbach. Copyright © 2019 Disney Enterprises, Inc./Pixar

'Toys That Go Bump in the Night' written by Lisa Marsoli. Copyright © 2019 Disney Enterprises, Inc./Pixar

'Rocket Launchers' written by Kate Egan. Copyright © 2019 Disney Enterprises, Inc./Pixar

'Woody's Quest for a Date' written by Lisa Marsoli. Copyright © 2019 Disney Enterprises, Inc./Pixar

'Toys in Paradise' written by Lisa Marsoli. Copyright © 2019 Disney Enterprises, Inc./Pixar

'So Long, Partner' written by Wendy Loggia. Copyright © 2019 Disney Enterprises, Inc./Pixar

Copyright © 2019 Disney Enterprises, Inc. and Pixar Animation Studios. All rights reserved.

Published by Scholastic Australia in 2019.

Scholastic Australia Pty Limited
PO Box 579 Gosford NSW 2250
ABN 11 000 614 577
www.scholastic.com.au

Part of the Scholastic Group
Sydney • Auckland • New York • Toronto • London • Mexico City • New Delhi
Hong Kong • Buenos Aires • Puerto Rico

All rights reserved. No part of this publication may be reproduced or transmitted in any form or by any means, electronic or mechanical, including photocopying, recording, storage in an information retrieval system, or otherwise, without the prior written permission of the publisher, unless specifically permitted under the Australian Copyright Act 1968 as amended.

ISBN 978-1-76066-872-3

Printed in China by RR Donnelley.

Scholastic Australia's policy, in association with RR Donnelley, is to use papers that are renewable and made efficiently from wood grown in responsibly managed forests, so as to minimise its environmental footprint.

10 9 8 7 6 5 4 3 2 1   19 20 21 22 23 / 1

Disney · PIXAR TOY STORY

A New Toy

Andy was a young boy with many toys. He loved playing with all of them, but his favourite was Sheriff Woody.

Woody was an old-fashioned cowboy doll with a pull string. He had been Andy's best friend since Andy was in kindergarten. He even had a special spot on Andy's bed where he slept each night.

Woody and Andy had all kinds of exciting adventures together. Andy had a playset of an old Western town. When Woody caught the bandits in town, Andy pulled his string.

'Reach for the sky!' Woody would say.

Once the good guys were all safe and the town was peaceful again, Andy would pull Woody's string. 'You're my favourite deputy,' the cowboy said.

One day, while Andy was playing with his toys, his mother called out, 'Your friends are going to be here any minute!'

'Okay,' Andy said. 'It's party time!'

He ran up the stairs to his room and dropped Woody on his bed. Then he went to the crib and picked up his little sister, Molly.

'See you later, Woody,' he called over his shoulder as he left the room.

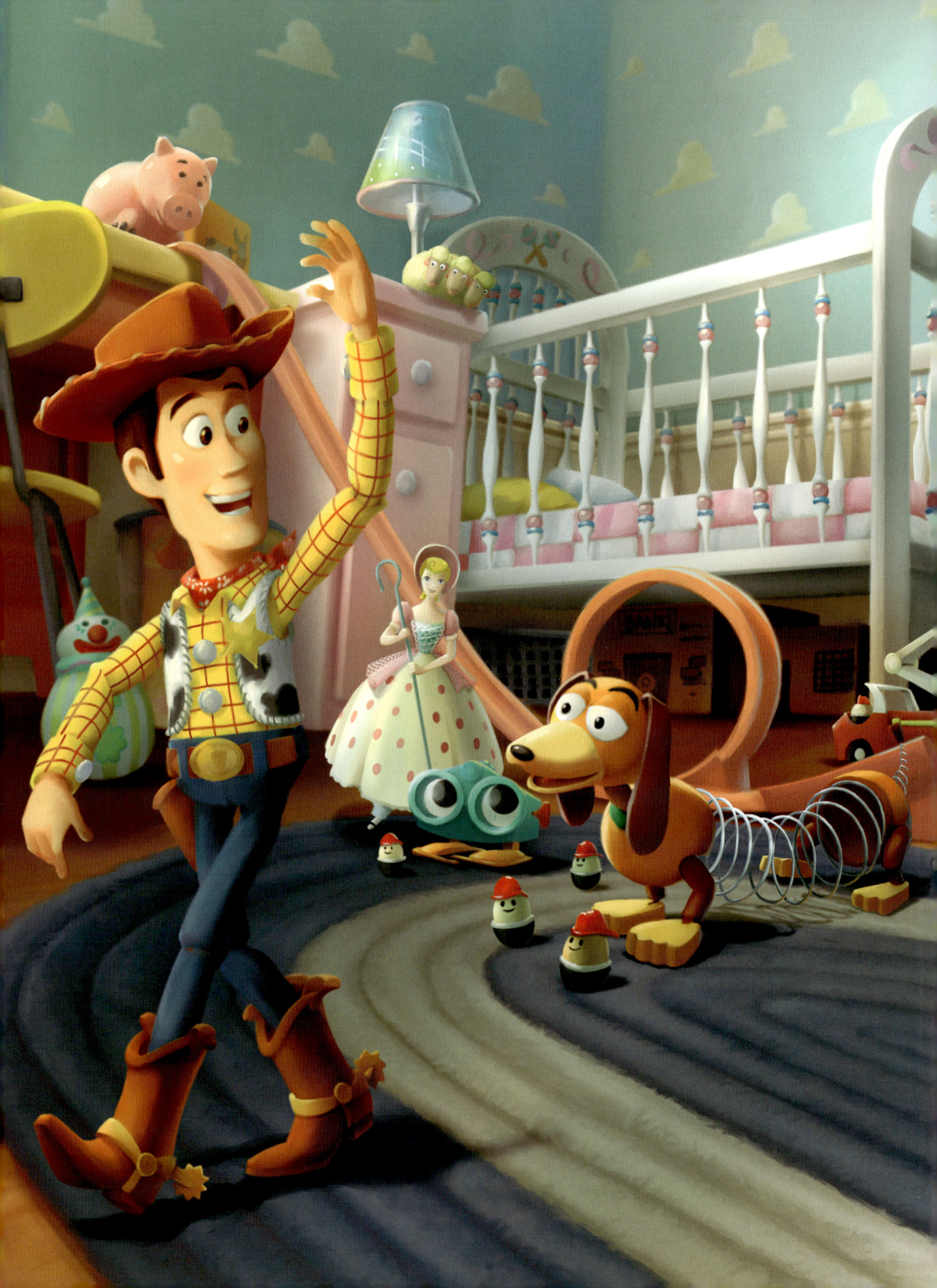

After Andy and Molly left, the room was quiet for a moment. Then, Woody sat up and rubbed his head.

'Pull my string,' he said. 'The birthday party's today?'

Woody waved at the other toys in the room. 'Okay, everybody, coast is clear!' he called out.

Slowly, the rest of Andy's toys came out of their spots in the closet, out from underneath the bed and out of the toy chest.

Woody dropped down from the bed onto the floor. All around him, toys stretched and chatted, something they could only do when there were no humans around to see them.

Woody looked around the room until he saw the toy he was trying to find. 'Hey, uh, Slinky?' Woody said as Slinky Dog approached. 'I've got some bad news.'

'Bad news?' Slinky Dog cried.

'*Shhh,*' Woody whispered. 'Just gather everyone up for a staff meeting. And look happy!'

When everyone was ready, Woody said, 'Okay, first item today . . . Has everyone picked a moving buddy?'

Andy and his family were moving to a new house in one week. Woody didn't want any toys to get lost or be left behind.

Woody made a couple more announcements. Then, when he couldn't hide the bad news any longer, he lowered his voice and said, 'Uh, minor note here. Andy's birthday party has been moved to today.'

'What?' all of the toys yelled at once.

Woody explained that this was because of the move.

But the toys were worried. Every time Andy got a present, they were afraid it would replace one of them!

'No-one's getting replaced,' Woody said.

Then Hamm announced that the kids were arriving.

Woody sent the Green Army Men downstairs with a baby monitor. They would radio up descriptions of each present as it was unwrapped.

Andy got a new lunch box and a board game, as well as a few other presents. Then his mother pulled out one last gift.

Before Sarge could give a full report, the baby monitor cut out. The other toys were frantic to know what the last present was!

Just then, Andy and his friends raced into the room. Andy dropped the last present on his bed. Then the kids ran back downstairs.

Woody was on the floor surrounded by the other toys. They looked at him, wondering what to do next.

'Let's all be polite and give whatever it is up there a nice, big, Andy's-room welcome,' he said.

Woody pulled himself up over the edge of the bed. The last present was a new toy. He was a bright plastic action figure in a spacesuit.

'Howdy,' Woody said, 'My name is Woody.'

'I'm Buzz Lightyear, space ranger,' the new toy said.

The other toys crept closer to meet Buzz. They were impressed by his laser and the wings that popped out of his backpack.

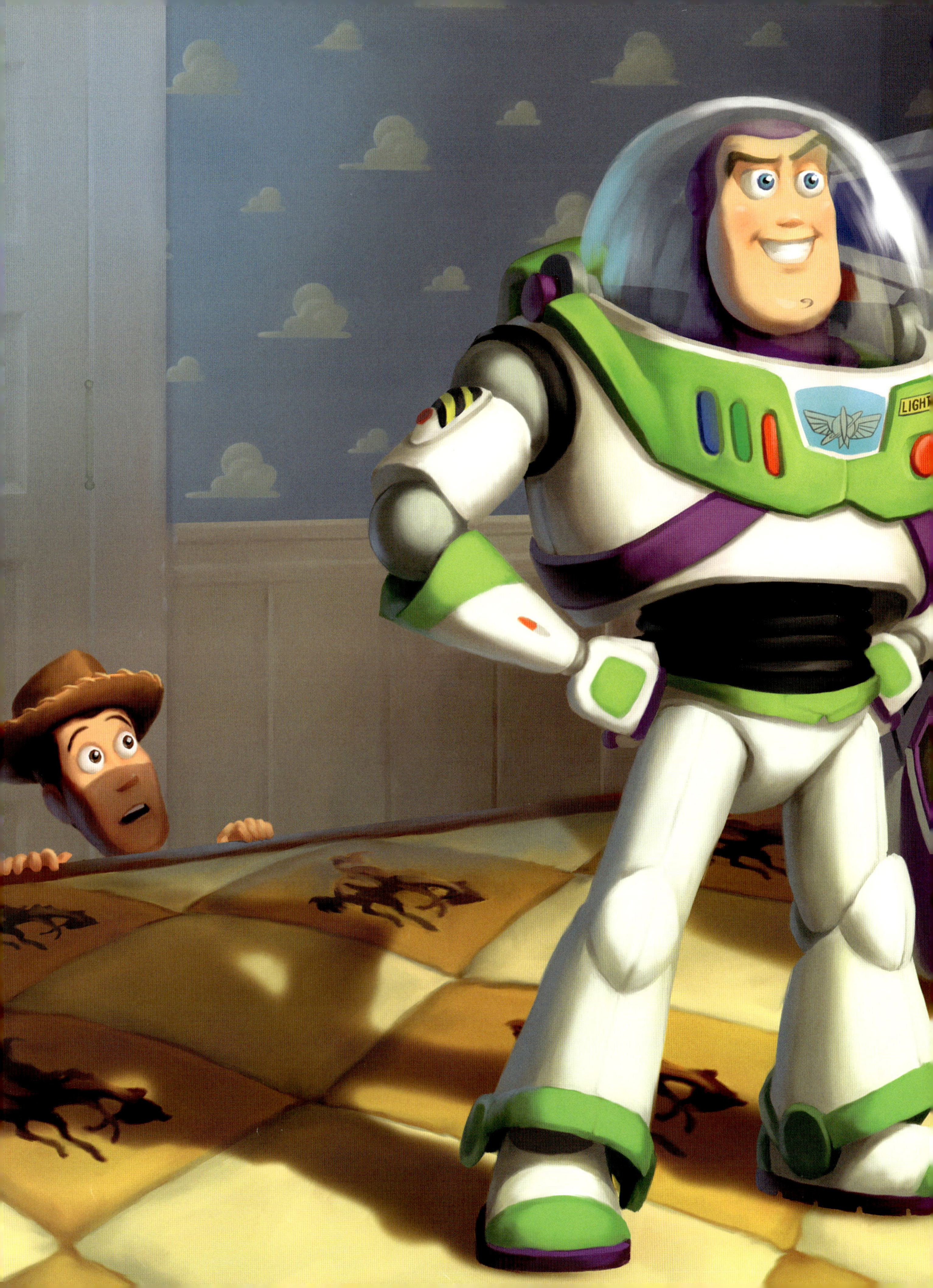
LIGHT

Buzz thought he was a real space ranger, sworn to protect the galaxy from the evil Emperor Zurg. The toys listened to his tales of adventure in awe. Then Buzz showed them how he could fly. He bounced off a rubber ball, rode around a racetrack loop and swung from a model airplane.

Woody didn't think Buzz was all that special. 'That wasn't flying,' he said. 'That was falling with style.'

But no-one listened to him. They were too busy helping Buzz repair his spaceship and trying his workout plan.

The other toys weren't the only ones who thought Buzz was a lot of fun. Suddenly, he had become Andy's favourite toy!

Woody looked on sadly as Andy traded his cowboy hat for a space helmet. He replaced his cowboy sheets with new Buzz Lightyear ones. And worst of all, Buzz took Woody's special spot on Andy's bed while Woody slept in the toy chest.

19

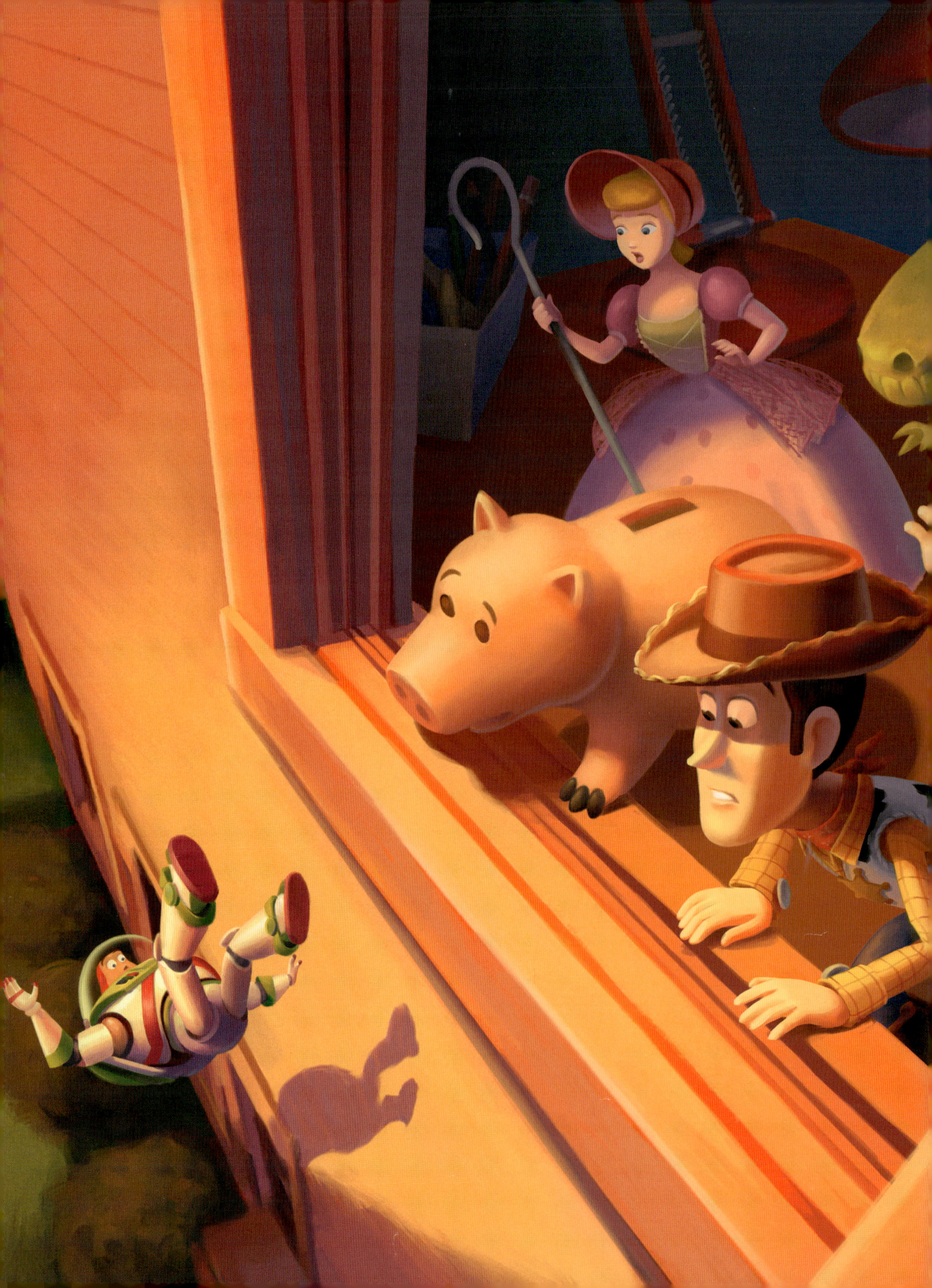

One evening, Andy's mum took him and Molly to Pizza Planet. She said he could bring one toy with him.

Woody wanted to be that toy! He planned to knock Buzz behind the desk where Andy couldn't find him. But instead, Buzz fell out the window!

The other toys glared at Woody. They thought he was trying to get rid of Buzz because he didn't like being replaced as Andy's favourite toy.

'Wait a minute,' Woody said. 'It was an accident. I can explain everything.'

Andy burst into the room before Woody could finish. 'Be right down,' he called out. 'I've got to get Buzz.'

When he couldn't find the space ranger anywhere, he grabbed Woody. Then he ran downstairs and hopped into the car.

Buzz watched Andy from underneath a shrub. As the car started up, he ran and leaped onto the car's bumper.

When Andy's mother pulled into a petrol station, Buzz jumped into the backseat with Woody.

'Buzz! You're alive!' Woody said excitedly. 'This is great! You can tell everyone that this was all just a big mistake.' Woody smiled.

Buzz wasn't happy, though. He tackled Woody so hard that they both fell out of the car.

They were so busy fighting that they didn't even notice Andy and his mum get back into the car until it drove off!

'Doesn't he realise that I'm not there?' Woody said as he watched the car disappear. 'I'm a lost toy!'

Buzz was talking into his wrist communicator, trying to call for help.

'You're a toy!' Woody yelled at the space ranger. 'You aren't the real Buzz Lightyear!'

Buzz shrugged. 'You're a sad, strange little man,' he said. Then he started to walk off.

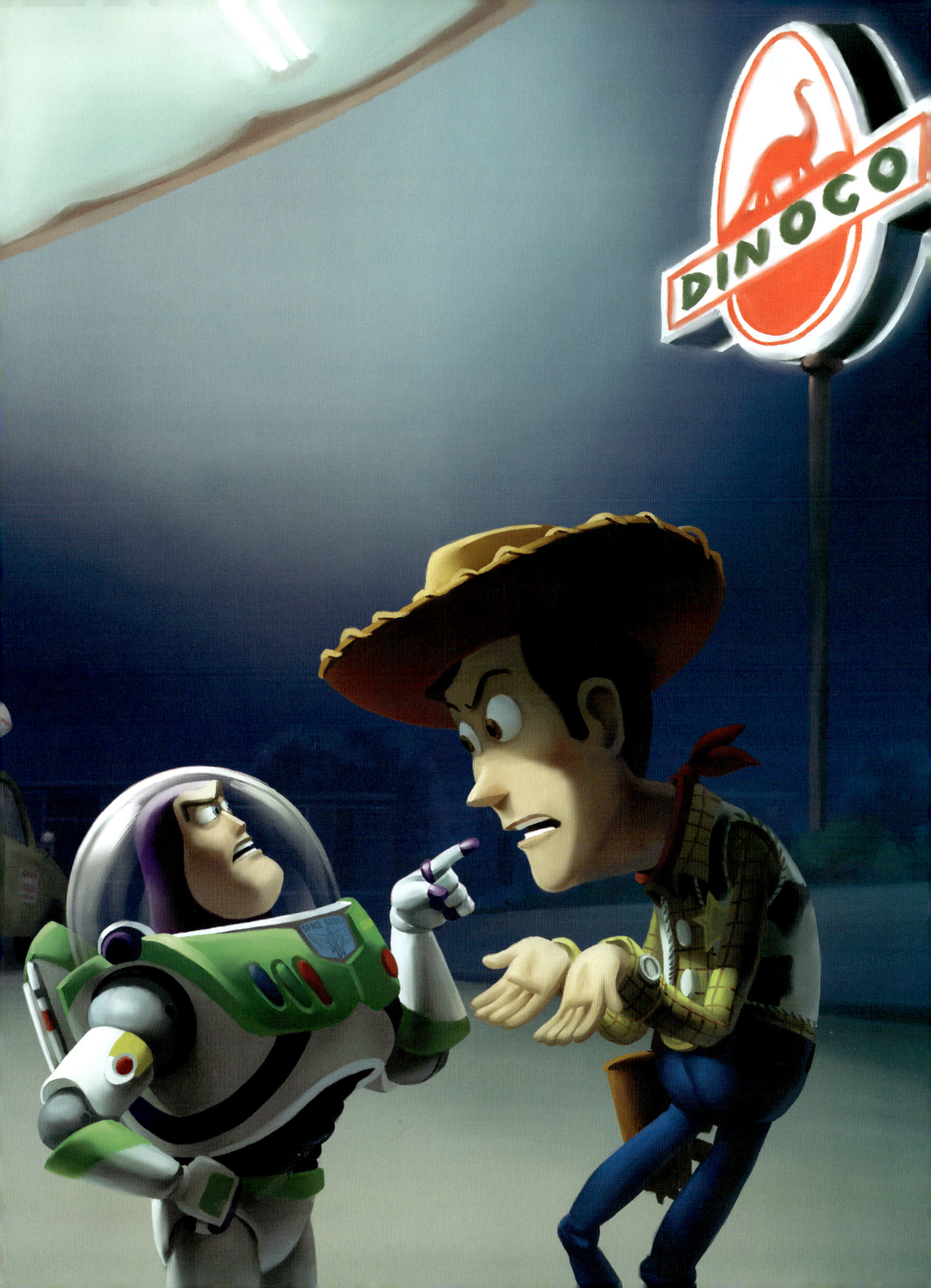
DINOCO

Woody wanted to let him go. But just then, a Pizza Planet delivery truck pulled into the petrol station.

Woody knew he couldn't return to Andy's room without Buzz. He told the space ranger he'd found a spaceship that would help him get home. The two toys climbed into the truck.

When they arrived at Pizza Planet, Woody led the space ranger over to Andy and his family. They needed to get close enough to hop in the basket of Molly's stroller.

'Okay, Buzz, get ready and . . . Buzz?' Woody turned around to see Buzz striding towards the Rocket Ship Crane Game. He thought it was a real spaceship.

Buzz climbed the game and fell into a pile of toy aliens. Woody followed.

Suddenly, Woody gasped. 'Sid!' he said. 'Get down!'

Sid was Andy's neighbour. He liked to destroy his toys for fun.

The claw started to move. It clamped on Buzz! Woody grabbed Buzz's foot to hold him down, but it was no use. They were both pulled into the air.

'All right!' Sid cheered as Woody and Buzz dropped into the prize slot. 'Double prizes!'

Sid reached into the door to the prize slot and picked up Woody and Buzz. He smiled at his two new toys.

'Let's go home and . . . play!' he said with a wicked laugh.

Woody knew they were doomed. They might be taken apart or blown up! But worst of all they might never see Andy again . . .

Disney · PIXAR
TOY STORY
Moving Day

Sid was Andy's next-door neighbour. He wasn't very nice to his toys. He'd take them apart, then attach one toy's head or legs to another's body.

Sid had won Woody the cowboy and Buzz Lightyear the space ranger in a game at Pizza Planet. Woody and Buzz had been at the restaurant looking for Andy.

As Woody looked around Sid's room, some of Sid's toys came out from their hiding places.

'They're gonna eat us, Buzz!' Woody yelled. 'Use your karate-chop action.'

Woody and Buzz managed to escape from Sid's toys. They ran out into the hallway and came face to face with Sid's dog, Scud. Woody ducked into a closet. Buzz hid in a dark room behind the door.

Suddenly, Buzz heard a voice saying, 'Calling Buzz Lightyear. This is Star Command.'

Buzz looked up at the TV. The voice was coming from an ad for Buzz Lightyear toys. It continued, 'The world's greatest superhero, now the world's greatest toy.'

Buzz stared in shock at the TV. He couldn't believe what he had just heard. He wondered if Woody had been right all along. Was he really just a toy?

The space ranger walked out of the room feeling sad. He looked out an open window at the blue sky and watched a bird fly by. He kept hearing Woody's voice in his head saying, 'You are a toy! You can't fly!'

He hung his head against the railing over the stairs. Then he had an idea. He would prove to Woody that he could fly. He *was* a space ranger!

Buzz climbed up and stood on the top of the railing. He opened his wings. Then he leaped.

'To infinity and beyond!' he called out.

He hung in the air for a moment and then started to fall. He crashed on the floor at the bottom of the stairs, breaking off his left arm.

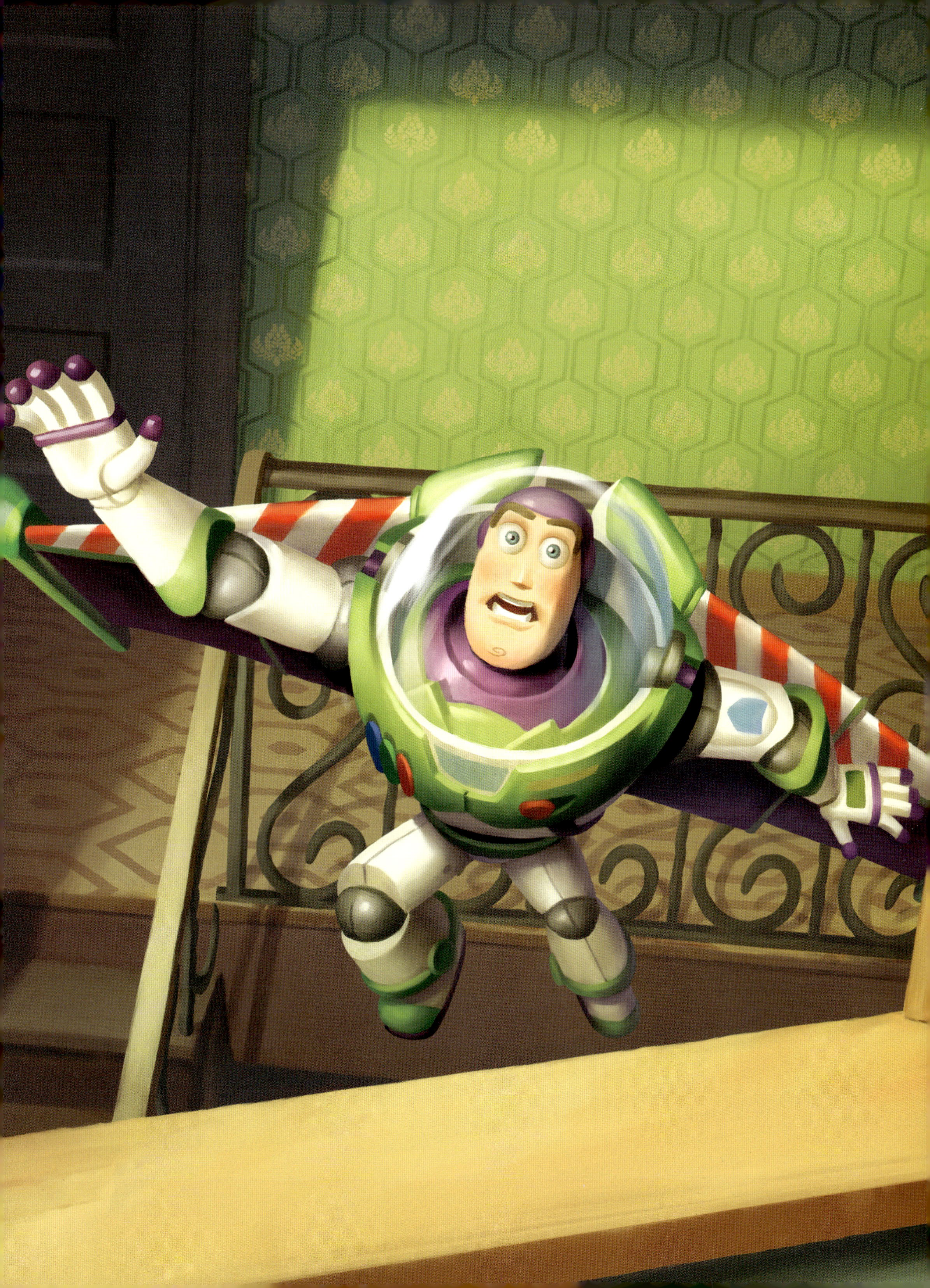

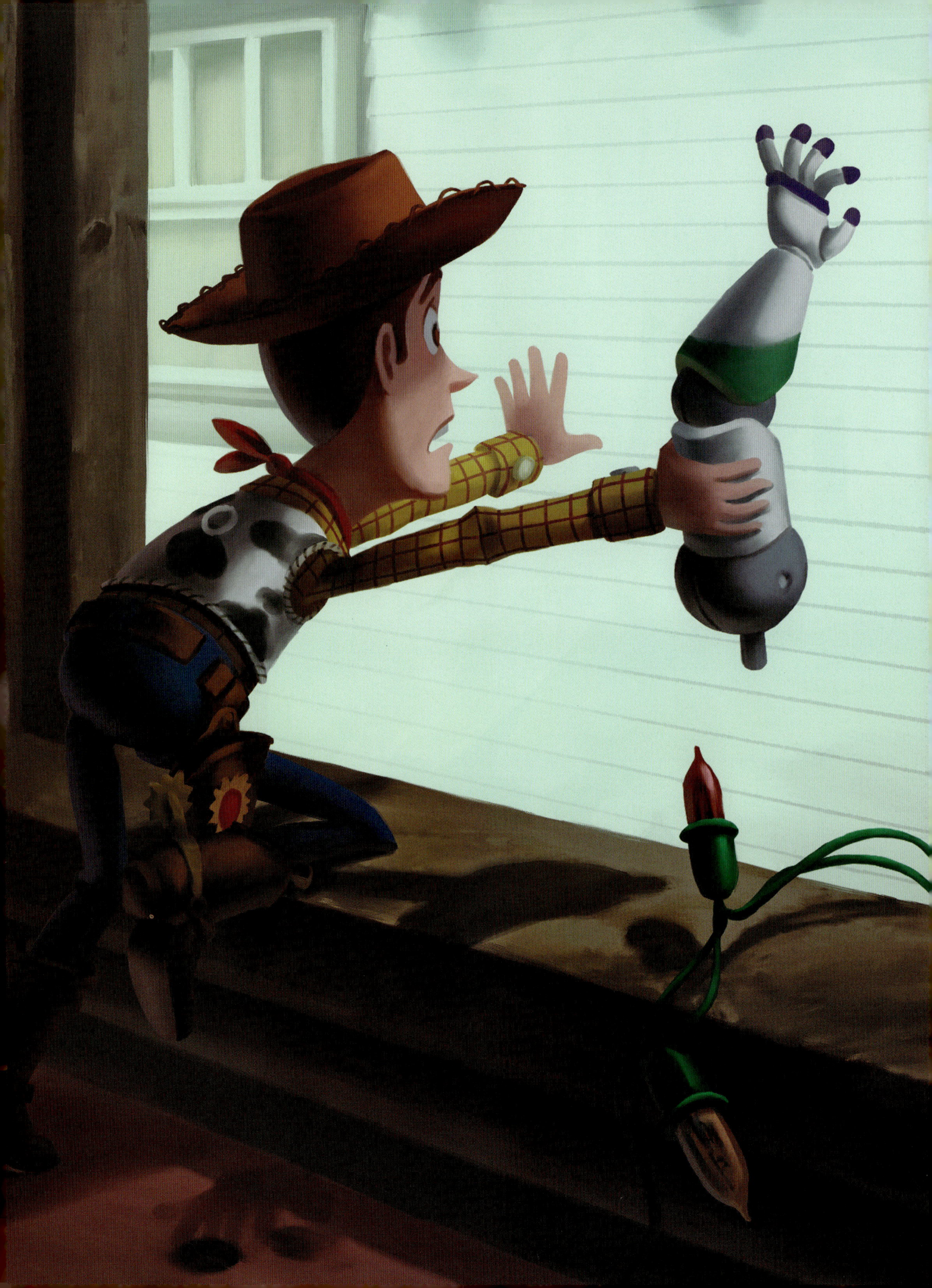

When Woody found him, Buzz was upset, but he understood that he was a toy.

Woody was desperate to get them both back to Andy's house. He ran to the open window and called out to the other toys, 'Hey, guys!'

Andy's toys appeared in the window next door. They were surprised Woody was there.

'Oh, boy, am I glad to see you guys,' Woody said. 'Here, catch this.' He tossed a string of Christmas lights over to them so he and Buzz could climb across.

But Buzz wouldn't move. Woody held out Buzz's broken arm to show that he was with him.

The other toys didn't believe Woody. They thought he had hurt their new friend.

Woody felt terrible. When he turned around to tell Buzz, he saw Sid's mutant toys closing in around the space ranger. Woody ran over to hold them back, but they took Buzz's arm and pushed the cowboy away.

Then, after a few minutes, the mutant toys stepped away from Buzz. They'd reattached his arm! Woody couldn't believe it.

Suddenly, the other toys scurried off. Sid was coming! Woody hid under a milk crate, but Buzz wouldn't move.

When Sid walked in the room, he held out a rocket. 'I've always wanted to put a spaceman into orbit,' he said. Then he taped the rocket to Buzz.

Sid was about to take Buzz outside when he saw a flash of lightning. 'Oh, no!' Sid cried. He looked at the rocket. The launch would just have to wait until tomorrow.

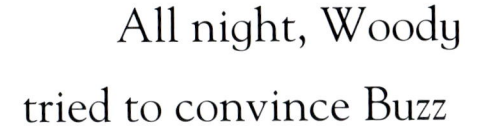

All night, Woody tried to convince Buzz to help him escape. He knew Andy's family was moving the next day and they had to get home.

But Buzz didn't care about going home. 'Andy's house, Sid's house, what's the difference?' he said. 'I'm just a little, insignificant toy.'

'Look,' Woody said, 'over in that house is a kid who thinks you are the greatest. And it's not because you're a space ranger, pal. It's because you're a toy! You're *his* toy.'

Woody tried to convince Buzz all night long. But Buzz didn't even move until he looked at the bottom of his boot. Andy had written his name there. Then Buzz knew what he had to do.

He walked over to Woody. 'Come on, Sheriff,' he said. 'There's a kid over in that house who needs us.'

Buzz helped Woody out from under the milk crate. But before they could escape, Sid woke up and grabbed Buzz. 'Time for liftoff!' he cried as he ran out of the room.

Woody asked Sid's toys to help him. 'We're going to have to break a few rules,' he said. 'But if it works, it'll help everybody.' The toys raced outside. Buzz was in position to be launched.

Sid got ready to light the rocket. Suddenly, he heard, 'Reach for the sky!' He looked around and saw Woody. He picked up the cowboy.

Then, Sid's toys came out from their hiding places in the backyard. Soon, Sid was surrounded by all the toys he had hurt.

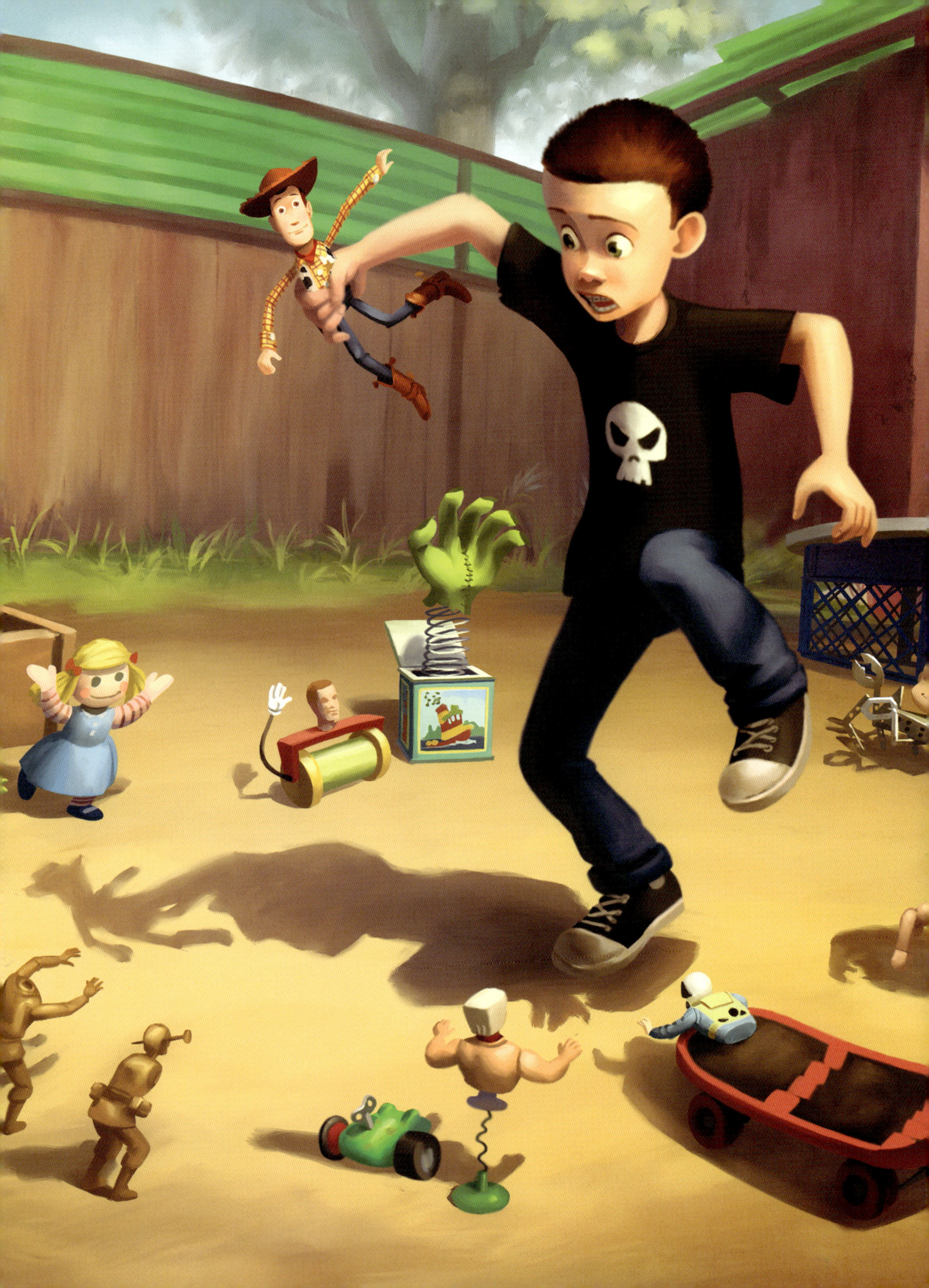

Sid looked at the toys around him. As each one came closer, he panicked more and more.

Woody kept speaking to Sid, which made the boy even more scared. 'From now on, you must take good care of your toys. Because if you don't we'll find out, Sid.' Then Woody leaned in close and pointed at Sid. 'So play nice!'

Sid screamed and dropped Woody. He ran into the house and slammed the door. The toys cheered!

Woody helped Buzz down off the launching pad. That's when he saw the moving truck pulling out of Andy's driveway.

Woody ran through the hole in the fence. But the rocket on Buzz's back got stuck. 'Just go,' Buzz called to Woody. 'I'll catch up.'

When Woody realised Buzz was stuck, he ran back to help him. The two toys ran down the street chasing the truck. Buzz was the first one there. He grabbed a loose strap and pulled himself up on the truck's bumper. Woody was right behind him.

'Come on,' Buzz said. 'You can do it, Woody!'

Woody grabbed the strap and started to pull himself up. But something grabbed his boot. It was Scud!

Buzz saved Woody by jumping onto Scud's head. But the truck was moving away quickly.

Woody climbed into the back of the van and rummaged through the boxes. The other toys didn't know what he was doing.

Finally, Woody found what he was looking for—RC Car! He sent RC out after Buzz. But Andy's other toys were upset with Woody. They still thought he'd hurt Buzz, so they pushed him out of the truck.

Then, they watched as Buzz and RC picked up Woody. Buzz had the remote control and was speeding towards the truck. The toys realised that it had all been a misunderstanding.

Slinky Dog stretched himself out as far as he could, but they still couldn't get close enough. Suddenly, RC started slowing down. His batteries had run out.

Woody watched sadly as the truck drove away. Then Buzz remembered the rocket on his back. They lit it and zoomed closer to the truck. RC landed easily in the back. But Woody and Buzz were launched into the sky.

Buzz snapped open his wings, and he and Woody broke free of the rocket.

'Buzz, you're flying!' Woody exclaimed.

'This isn't flying,' Buzz said. 'This is falling with style.'

The two toys flew towards Andy's car. They dropped through the open sunroof and landed safely on the backseat.

Andy turned and saw the cowboy and space ranger. 'Woody! Buzz!' he shouted. He was happy to have his two favourite toys back.

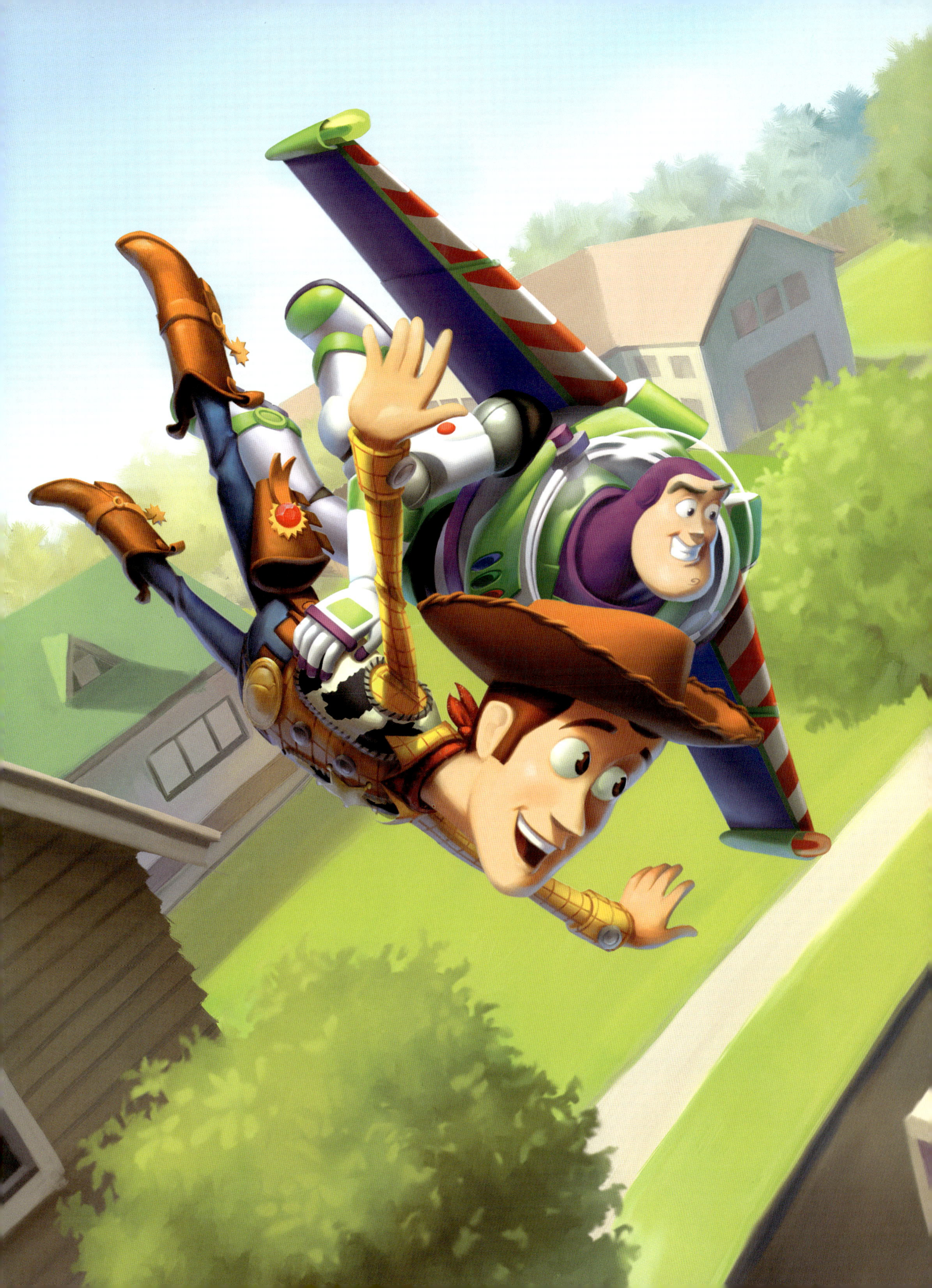

Woody and Buzz settled into Andy's new house with the rest of his toys. They were happy to be home.

When Christmas rolled around, the toys sat near the baby monitor to listen as Andy opened his gifts.

'You're not worried are you?' Woody asked Buzz.

'No,' Buzz replied nervously. 'Are you?'

'Now, Buzz, what could Andy possibly get that is worse than you?' Woody teased.

They listened as the first present was opened.

Woof! Woof!

'Wow! A puppy!' Andy cried.

Buzz and Woody looked at each other and laughed. At least it wasn't a toy!

Disney · PIXAR
TOY STORY 2

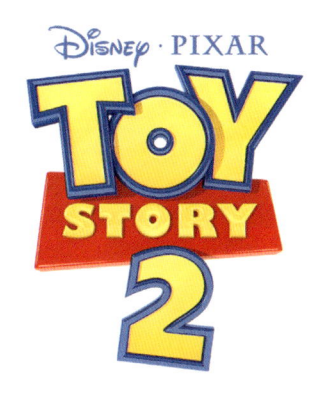

Woody's Big Adventure

'Hey, Woody! Ready to go to cowboy camp?' Andy asked.

Woody the cowboy doll was very excited about camp. He'd been looking forward to it for weeks.

Andy grabbed Woody and Buzz Lightyear the space ranger, his two favourite toys. 'Never tangle with the unstoppable duo of Woody and Buzz Lightyear!' he exclaimed, linking the toys' arms together.

Just then, there was a loud *RIIIPPP*! Woody's shoulder had a tear in it.

Andy's mum suggested fixing Woody on the way to camp, but Andy shook his head sadly. 'No, just leave him.'

'I'm sorry, honey,' said his mum. 'But you know, toys don't last forever.' She put Woody up on a high shelf.

Woody looked out the window as Andy left without him. He felt even worse when he discovered Wheezy, a toy penguin who'd been put on the same shelf months ago after his squeaker broke. Woody wondered if that was *his* future, too.

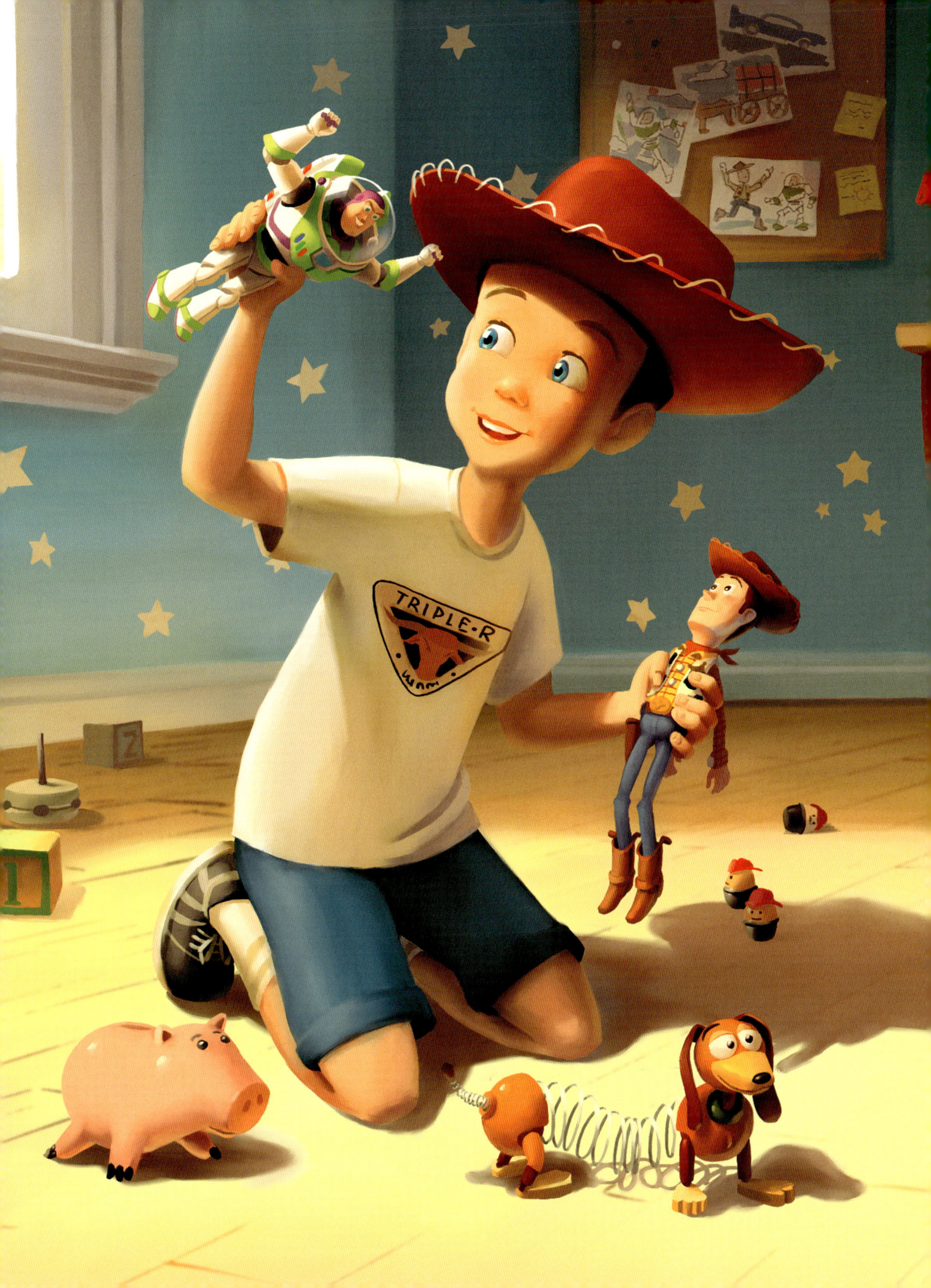
TRIPLE-R

The next morning, the toys spotted something terrifying. Andy's mum had put up a sign for a garage sale!

She looked around Andy's room for items to sell. The toys all watched in horror as she picked up Wheezy.

Woody waited until Andy's mum left the room, then he whistled for Andy's dog, Buster. Together, they snuck outside and rescued Wheezy. But as they headed back to safety, Woody tumbled to the ground. With his injured arm, he couldn't hold onto Buster's collar.

One of the sale shoppers saw Woody and picked him up. Then he smiled with excitement. 'Oh, I found him!' he said.

The man grabbed some other items to buy, hiding Woody in between them. But Andy's mother saw the cowboy. She told the man that Woody wasn't for sale.

'I'm sorry,' she said. 'It's an old family toy.' She took Woody and locked him up in the cash box.

As soon as she turned around, the man pried open the box and stole Woody! From their upstairs window, the other toys watched in shock.

Buzz quickly jumped out the window and slid down the drainpipe to rescue his friend. But he was too late. Buzz watched the man's car drive away. The license plate read LZTYBRN.

The man brought Woody home and put him in a glass case. Then he put on a chicken suit.

'You, my little cowboy friend, are going to make me big buck, buck, bucks!' the man said. He flapped his wings and walked out.

Woody knew the man was the owner of Al's Toy Barn. He'd seen him wearing the chicken suit on a commerical for the store.

Woody pushed open the door to the glass case and ran to the door. But he couldn't get out of the apartment.

Suddenly, a toy horse galloped over and a cowgirl hugged him tightly. '*Yee-hah!* It's really you!' she shouted.

She danced Woody around and pulled his string. Then she put her ear to his chest and listened to his voice box say, 'There's a snake in my boot!'

'Ha! It is you!' the cowgirl exclaimed. Her name was Jessie. She introduced Woody to the horse, Bullseye, and a toy still in its box—the Prospector.

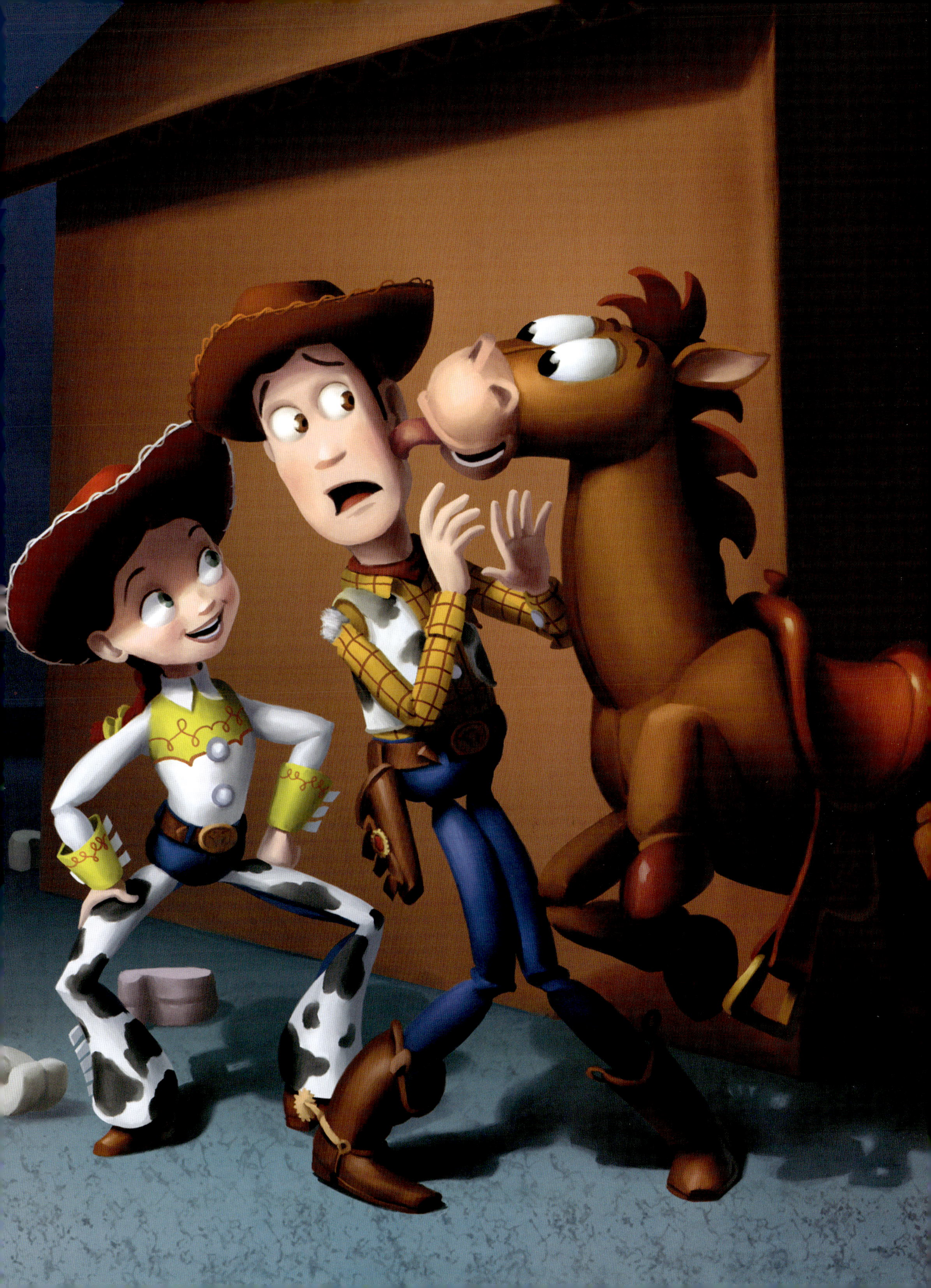

'We've waited countless years for this day,' the Prospector said. 'It's good to see you, Woody!'

'Hey, how do you know my name?' Woody asked.

'Why, you don't know who you are, do you?' said the Prospector.

Bullseye turned on the lights to reveal a room filled with things that had Woody's picture on them. Then Jessie showed Woody an old television show called *Woody's Roundup*. Woody was the star!

Meanwhile, back in Andy's room, Buzz and the other toys had figured out who had taken Woody. Buzz came up with a plan to rescue his friend.

'Woody once risked his life to save me,' Buzz told the others. 'I couldn't call myself his friend if I weren't willing to do the same.'

He and some of the toys set off for the store. 'We'll be back before Andy gets home,' Buzz told the toys staying behind. 'To Al's Toy Barn and beyond!'

At Al's apartment, Woody was watching episodes of *Woody's Roundup.* When the show was over, Woody, Jessie and Bullseye hopped on a spinning record and ran around in circles. *'Whoo-eee!'* Jessie cried. 'We're a complete set!'

'Now, it's on to the museum!' declared the Prospector.

Woody paused. 'What museum?' he asked.

The Prospector told him that as a complete set they were valuable toys. Al planned to sell them to a museum in Japan for a lot of money.

'I can't go to Japan,' Woody said. 'I gotta get back home to my owner, Andy!'

Jessie gasped. 'He still has an owner!' she cried. She shook her head. 'I can't do storage again.'

'The museum's only interested in the collection if you're in it, Woody,' the Prospector said. 'Without you, we go back into storage.'

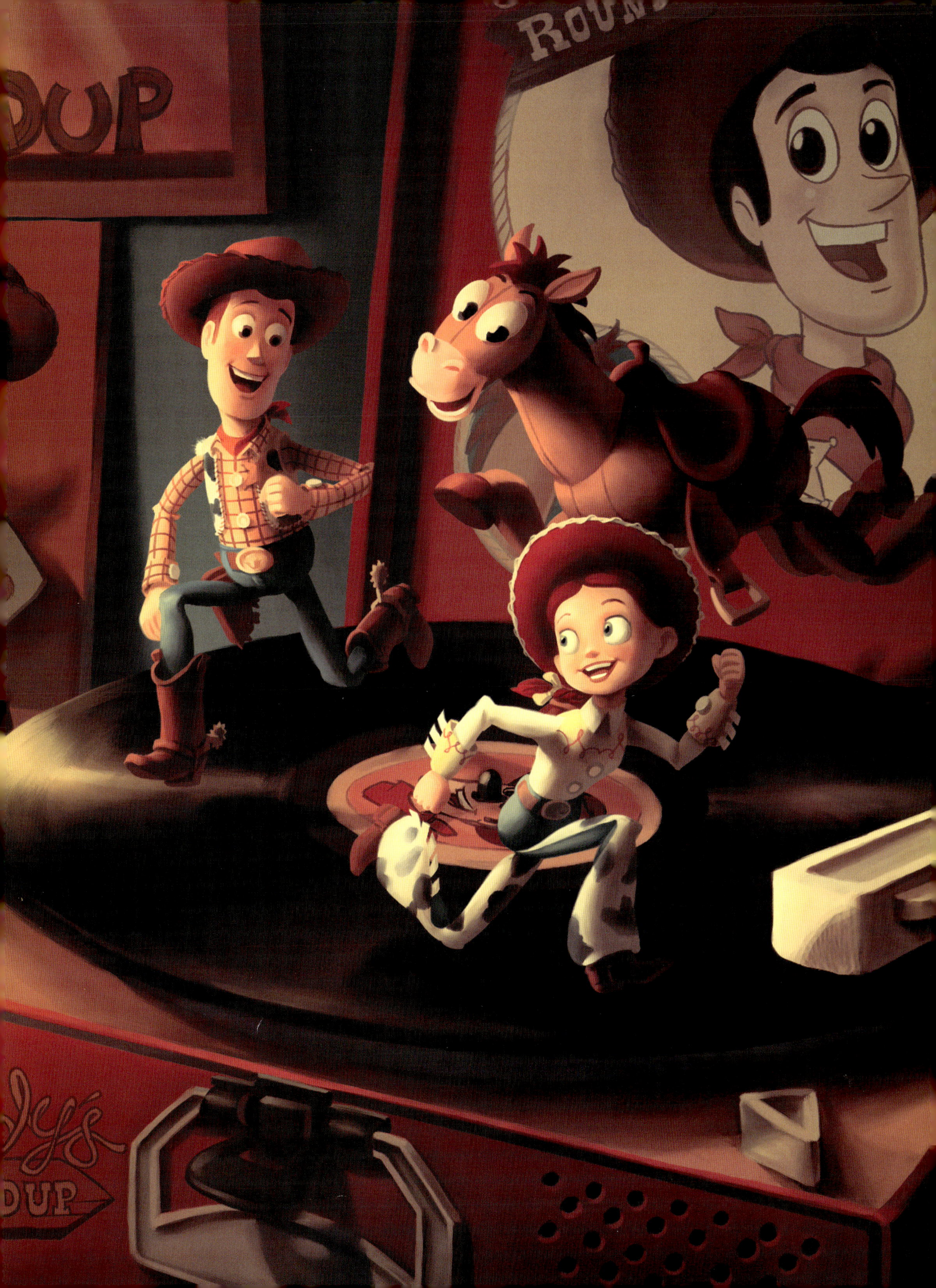
ROUN
DUP
DUP

Meanwhile, Buzz and his team were almost at Al's Toy Barn. They had one last street to cross, and it was a busy one.

Buzz noticed a pile of orange traffic cones. He instructed everyone to grab one and put it on. Then, slowly, they started to cross the street. Buzz called out directions as they went. 'Go!' he said. Then, 'Drop! I said drop!'

A car skidded to a halt. *Beep! Beep!* Soon the street was filled with skidding, honking cars, all trying to avoid the moving cones.

Luckily, the toys made it safely across.

Inside the store, the toys looked at the many aisles of shiny new toys.

'Whoa,' said Slinky. 'How are we going to find Woody?'

'Look for Al,' Buzz instructed. 'We find Al, we find Woody.'

Buzz walked down an aisle full of brand-new Buzz Lightyear toys. He gasped when he saw their fancy new utility belts.

'I could use one of those,' he said. As Buzz reached out to touch a belt, the new Buzz Lightyear stopped him.

Buzz tried to walk away, but the new Buzz tackled him and put him in a box. Then the new Buzz ran off to join Andy's toys.

Back at Al's apartment, Jessie was upset that Woody wouldn't go to the museum.

'I'm still Andy's toy,' he told her. 'If you knew him, you'd understand.'

'Let me guess,' Jessie said sadly. 'Andy's a real special kid and you're his best friend, and when Andy plays with you it's like . . . you feel like you're alive.'

Woody stared at Jessie in wonder. 'How did you know that?'

'Because Emily was just the same,' Jessie replied. 'She was my whole world. You never forget kids like Emily or Andy. But they forget you.'

Woody felt terrible. 'Jessie, I—' he started.

'Just go,' she said.

Woody turned and walked away. He didn't know what to do. He didn't want to leave his new friends, but he couldn't help thinking about the old ones.

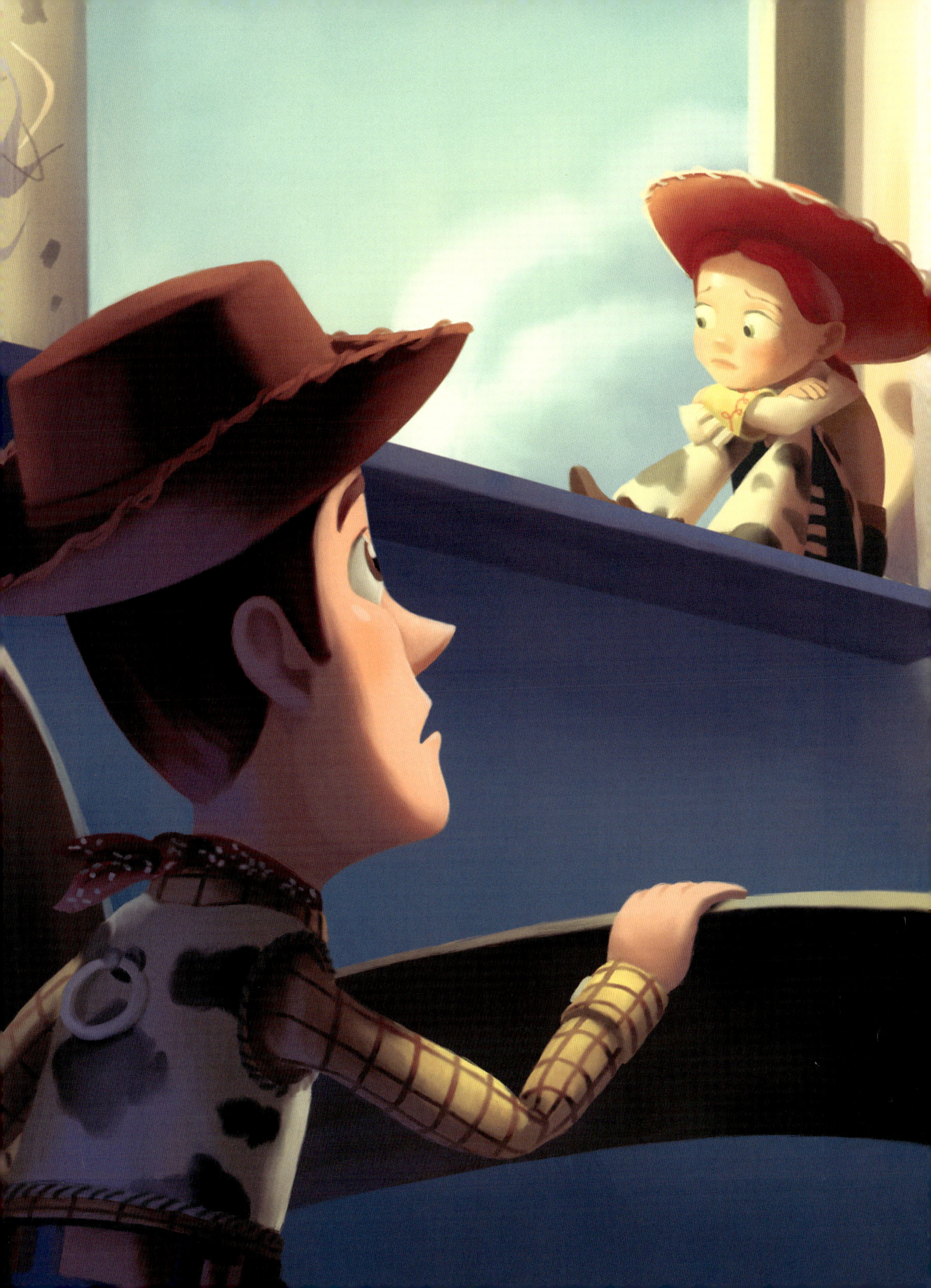

Meanwhile, the new Buzz and Andy's toys had gone to Al's apartment building. The new Buzz pulled the grate off an air vent for the toys to crawl through. 'Come on,' he said. 'We've got no time to lose.'

Since he thought he was a real space ranger, he tried to fly up to the top floor through the elevator shaft! Luckily, the elevator arrived just in time and carried everyone up on its roof instead.

When the toys reached the apartment they were excited to see Woody.

New Buzz grabbed Woody. Slinky wrapped Jessie and Bullseye up in his coils, and Hamm jumped on the Prospector's box.

'Hold it right there!' a voice said suddenly. It was the real Buzz!

The real Buzz tried to get Woody to leave with them, but Woody didn't want to go.

'I can't abandon these guys,' Woody explained. 'They need me to get into the museum.'

Woody told his friends about the old TV show *Woody's Roundup*. He wanted them to understand.

'Woody, you're not a collector's item!' Buzz cried. 'You are a toy!'

'This is my only chance,' said Woody.

'To do what?' Buzz asked angrily. 'To watch kids from behind glass and never be loved again? Some life.'

Buzz turned to leave with the new Buzz and Andy's other toys.

Woody looked sadly between the old TV show and Andy's name on the bottom of his boot. He loved Andy. But he didn't want to be forgotten when Andy was all grown up. Wouldn't it be better to be loved by all the visitors at the museum?

Disney · PIXAR
TOY STORY 2

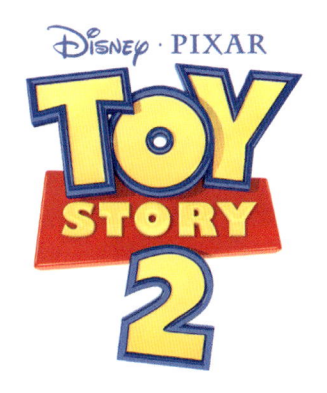

A Wild Ride

Woody the cowboy doll watched his friends leave through the air vent. They'd come to bring him home. A man named Al had stolen Woody to sell him and the rest of the Roundup Gang—Jessie the cowgirl, Bullseye the horse and the Prospector—to a museum in Japan. Woody was ready to go. He was afraid that if he went home Andy would grow up and forget about him. But his friends didn't understand.

Suddenly, Woody realised that he couldn't stop Andy from growing up, but he didn't want to miss seeing it, either.

'Buzz! Wait! I'm coming with you!' Woody shouted.

Woody turned to his new friends and urged them to come with him. But the Prospector blocked the vent.

'No hand-me-down cowboy doll is gonna screw it up for me now!' the Prospector said.

He didn't want Woody to leave. Without Woody, they couldn't be sold to the museum.

Just then, the toys heard footsteps approaching. They quickly moved back to their places.

Al hurried into the room and packed the Roundup Gang in his suitcase. Then he ran out the door. He was late for his flight to Japan. He wanted to sell the toys as quickly as possible.

Andy's toys and the new Buzz Lightyear they had met on the search for Woody all watched in panic from inside the vent.

'Quick! To the elevator!' shouted the real Buzz, hoping to catch Al.

But when they got there, an evil Emperor Zurg toy stood on the elevator roof. Zurg was Buzz Lightyear's enemy. He had seen the real Buzz escape from Al's Toy Barn and followed him to the apartment building.

Zurg attacked with his blaster, and the new Buzz fired back with his laser. Rex was too scared to watch. As the dinosaur turned away, his tail accidentally knocked Zurg off the elevator roof!

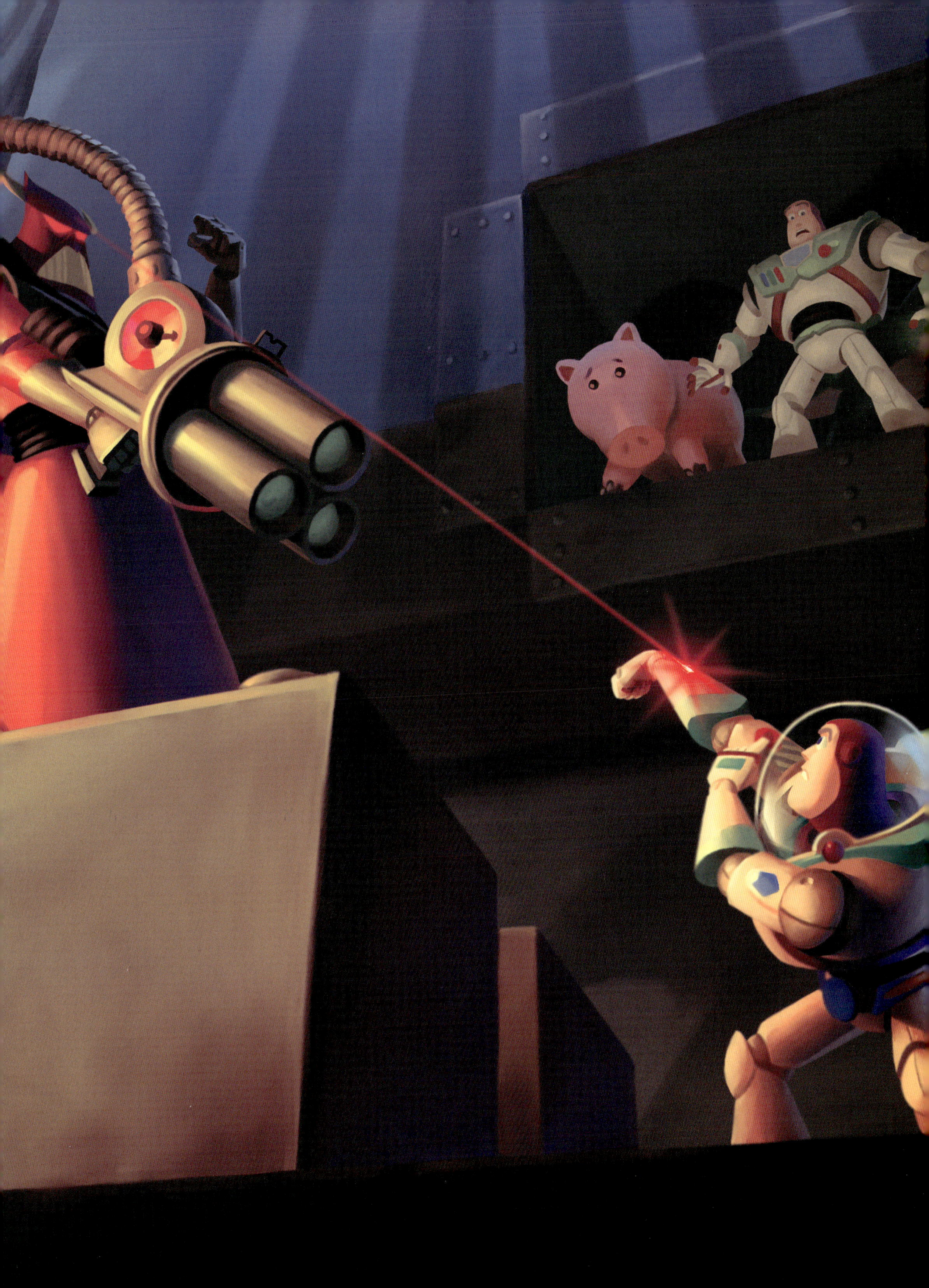

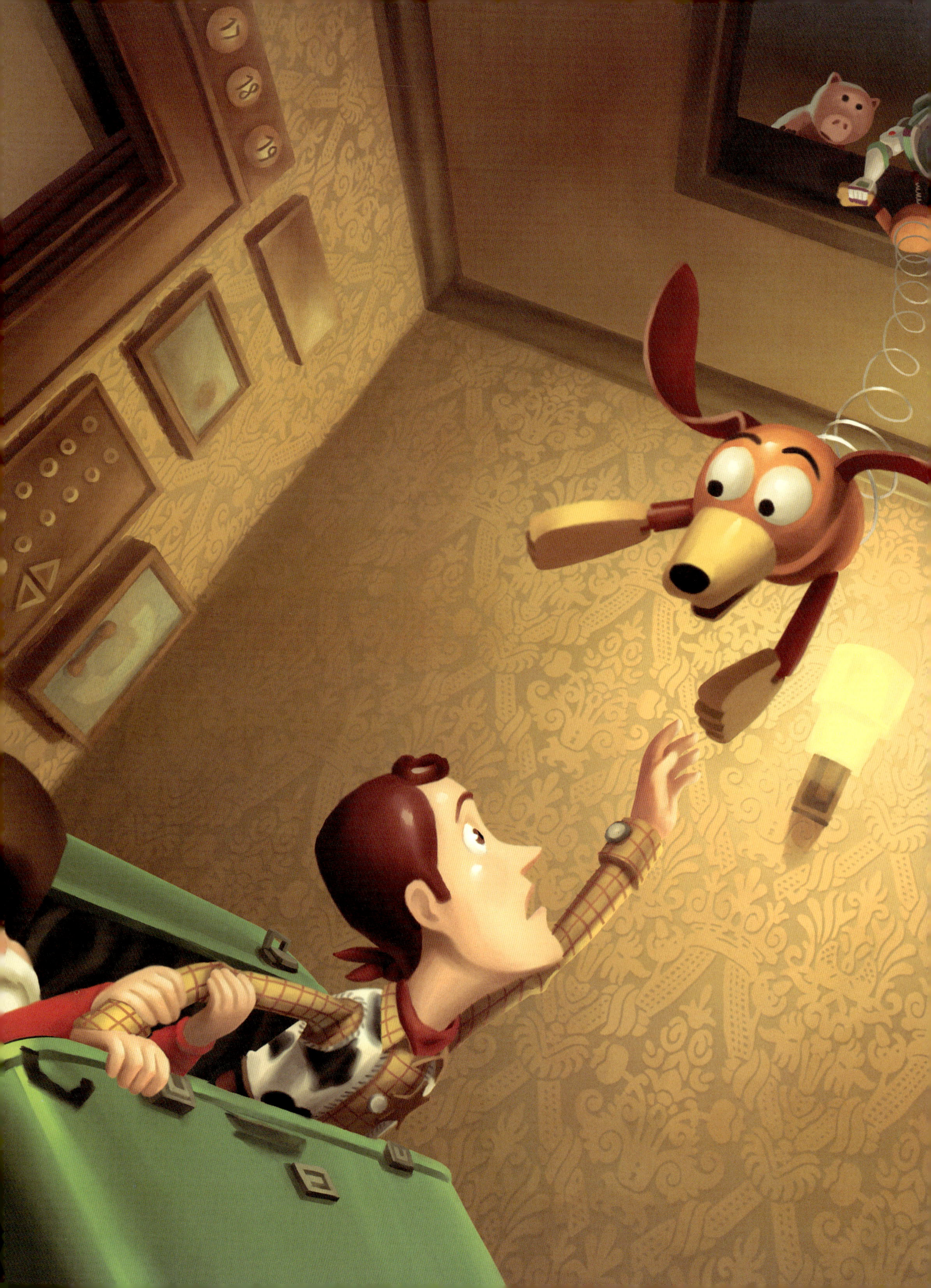
17
18
19

With Zurg out of the way, the toys lifted the elevator roof. Al was impatiently waiting to get to the ground floor.

'C'mon,' he muttered. 'C'mon, c'mon.'

Buzz held onto Slinky's legs, and Slinky stretched down to Al's case to undo the latches. Woody popped out of the case and grabbed hold of Slinky's paw.

Just as Slinky Dog started to pull Woody up, the Prospector grabbed Woody's arm tightly and yanked him back inside the case.

Ding!

'Ah, finally!' Al exclaimed as the elevator reached the ground floor. As the doors slid open, the Prospector shoved Woody back down in the case.

Al hurried out of the elevator and ran outside.

Inside the elevator, Andy's toys dropped down from the roof. They watched Al leave. Then the toys ran to the doors, squeezing through them just before they closed.

By the time Andy's toys were outside, Al had already driven off.

They spotted a Pizza Planet delivery truck—and the door was open! The new Buzz went back to Al's Toy Barn. But everyone else hopped into the truck.

Buzz took control of the wheel. 'Slink, you take the pedals,' he said. 'Rex, you navigate.'

Rex stood on the dashboard and looked for Al's car. 'He's at a red light!' he suddenly shouted. 'We can catch him.'

Three squeeze-toy aliens hung from the rearview mirror. When the car wouldn't move, they said, 'Use the wand of power.'

Hamm pushed the gears and the truck sped off.

'Rex, which way?' asked Buzz.

'Right,' said Rex. 'I mean left. No, right. *Your* right!'

They swerved through traffic and followed Al all the way to the airport.

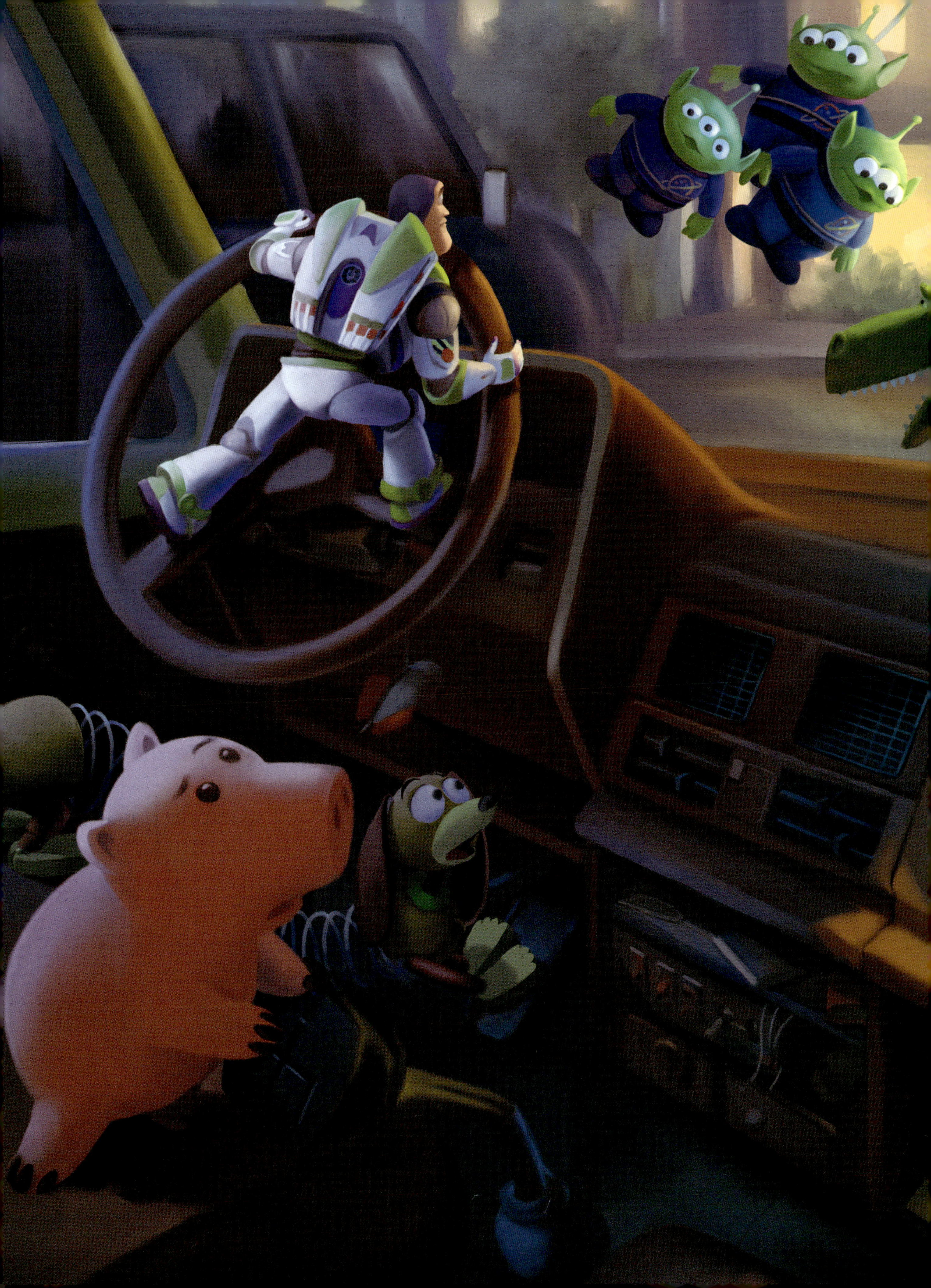

At the airport, the toys didn't know how they'd get through the crowd without anyone seeing them.

Then Buzz spotted a pet carrier. The toys piled inside, sticking their legs through the small openings in the bottom so they could walk.

'Ahh! Someone's coming!' cried Rex.

It was a little girl. 'Oh, a puppy!' she squealed.

Slinky Dog barked a few times to scare her off.

Buzz gave Slinky a thumbs-up. The barking had worked!

At the counter, Al was arguing with the ticket agent.

'I am *not* checking it,' he told the agent. He didn't want to lose sight of the suitcase with the Roundup Gang toys.

But he finally gave in. The ticket agent took the suitcase.

Still in the pet carrier, Andy's toys followed the green suitcase into the baggage area.

The toys gasped. There were hundreds of suitcases moving in all different directions. How would they ever find Woody?

'There's the case!' yelled Slinky.

'No, *there's* the case,' said Hamm, spotting another green one that looked exactly the same.

The toys split up. When Buzz opened a suitcase, the Prospector jumped up and punched him.

'Hey! No-one does that to my friend!' Woody yelled at the Prospector. Woody grabbed him and the two started fighting. Woody's arm was torn in the same spot it had been earlier. Al had stitched him up so he'd be in perfect shape for the museum.

Buzz raced to the rescue.

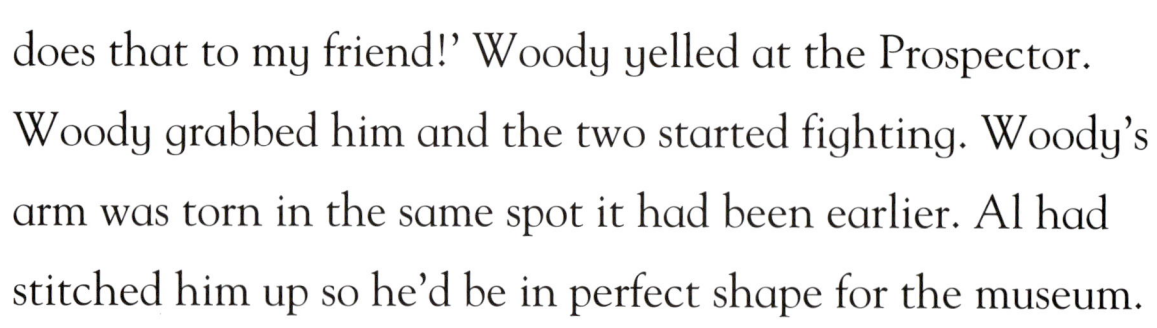

Woody looked at the Prospector and grinned. 'I think it's about time you learned the true meaning of "playtime",' he said.

Then Woody and Buzz strapped the Prospector to a pink backpack. He moved out of the baggage area and a little girl picked him up.

'Ooh! A big, ugly man doll,' said the girl. 'He needs a makeover.'

The Prospector was scared. 'I've got to get out of here,' he said. But it was no use.

Back inside the baggage area, Bullseye had freed himself from the green case, but Jessie was stuck.

'Woody, help!' she cried.

The toys watched as the case was loaded onto a cart. Woody and Buzz jumped on Bullseye's back.

'Ride like the wind, Bullseye!' Woody shouted.

They raced after the cart. Woody scrambled onto the cart, but it was too late. The green case was already being loaded onto a plane. Woody jumped into another bag so that he could get on that plane. He had to save Jessie!

Once he was on board, Woody jumped out and ran to the green suitcase.

'Excuse me, ma'am,' Woody said to Jessie. 'But I believe you're on the wrong flight.' He grinned.

Jessie's eyes lit up. 'Woody!' she cried and hugged him.

'Come on, Jess,' said Woody. 'It's time to take you home.'

Just then, the plane door shut. They were trapped!

The plane started to move. They had to get off!

They found a hatch and crawled down to the plane's wheels. It was hard to stay on, and Woody slipped. Luckily, Jessie grabbed his arm in time.

Woody's hat flew off but it was caught—by Buzz! He and Bullseye were riding alongside the plane. Woody was so happy to see him.

Then the cowboy came up with a daring plan. First he told Buzz to get behind the plane's tyres. Then Woody used his pull string as a lasso and looped the end of it around a bolt.

'Jessie!' he shouted. 'Let go of the plane!'

'What? Are you crazy?' Jessie shouted back.

But she trusted Woody, so she let go of the plane. Holding onto each other, the pair swung down and under the plane. Woody's pull string unhooked from the bolt. They dropped onto Bullseye's back behind Buzz!

'Nice roping, cowboy,' Buzz said to Woody.

Jessie hugged Woody. 'That was definitely Woody's finest hour!'

Woody smiled and looked at his friends. 'Let's go home.'

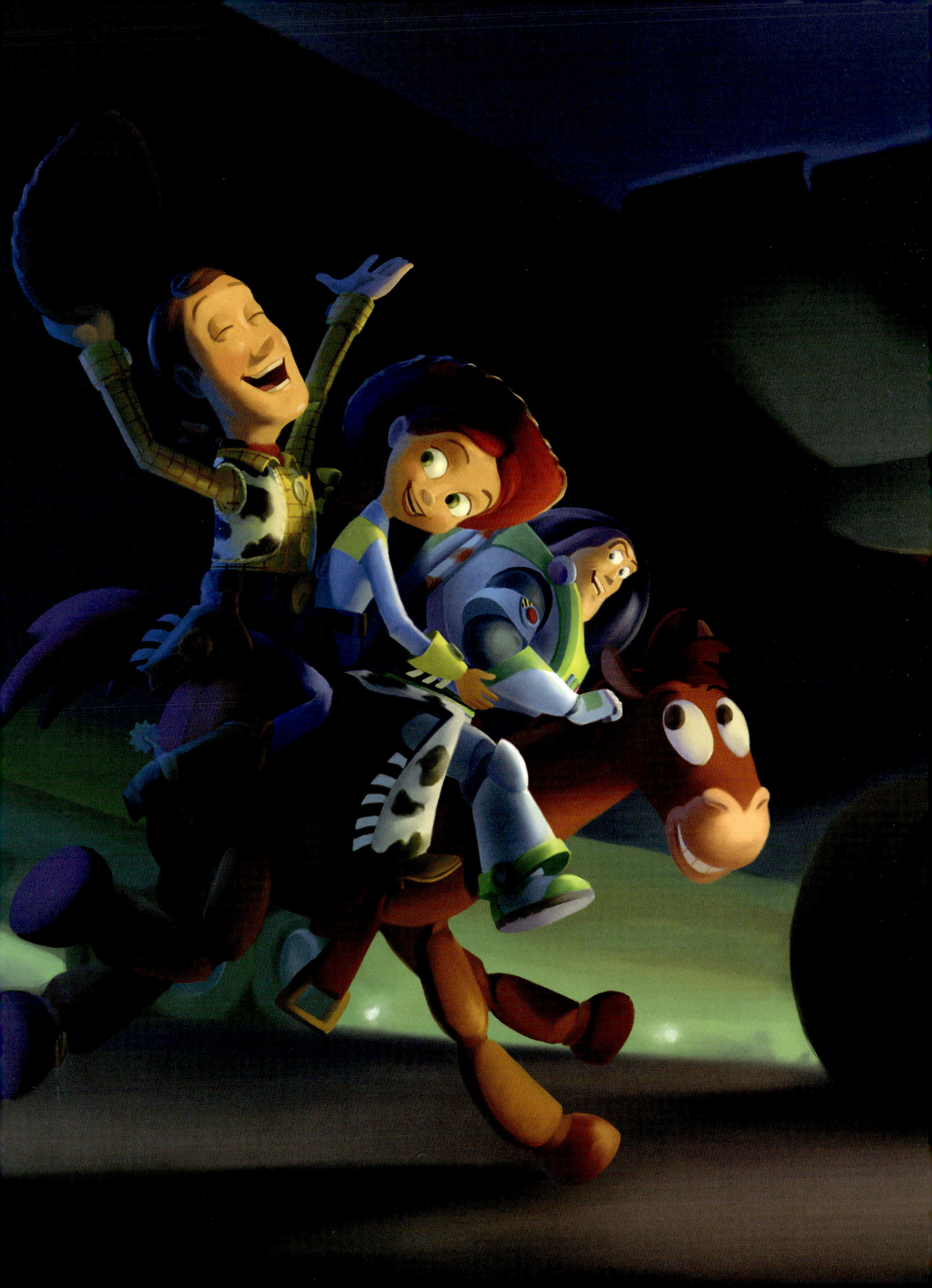

When Andy returned from Cowboy Camp, he was happy to see his toys. Jessie and Bullseye had joined the rest of the toys to welcome him home.

'Oh, wow! New toys!' Andy said when he saw the cowgirl and the horse. 'Thanks, Mum!'

Buzz looked at Woody and smiled. 'You still worried?' he asked.

'About Andy? No,' he said. 'It'll be fun while it lasts.'

D I S N E Y · PIXAR

TOY STORY

Toys That Go Bump in the Night

Andy was at a friend's house for a sleepover, so the toys had the whole night to themselves. 'What do you feel like doing?' Woody the cowboy asked the other toys.

'How about a spelling bee?' suggested Mr Spell.

'Nah, you always win,' Hamm the piggy bank replied.

'What about a game of hide-and-seek?' suggested Slinky Dog.

'I'd rather not,' Rex the dinosaur said nervously. He didn't like small, dark places.

Suddenly, rain began pelting the windows. A streak of lightning lit up the sky.

Rex shuddered. 'Oh, no!' he cried.

'Reminds me of the newest Buzz Lightyear video game,' the space ranger said. 'It starts with a storm forcing me to crash-land on a hostile planet. You don't even want to know what happens next.'

'Yes, we do,' said Bo Peep. 'Telling scary stories is the perfect thing to do on a stormy night.'

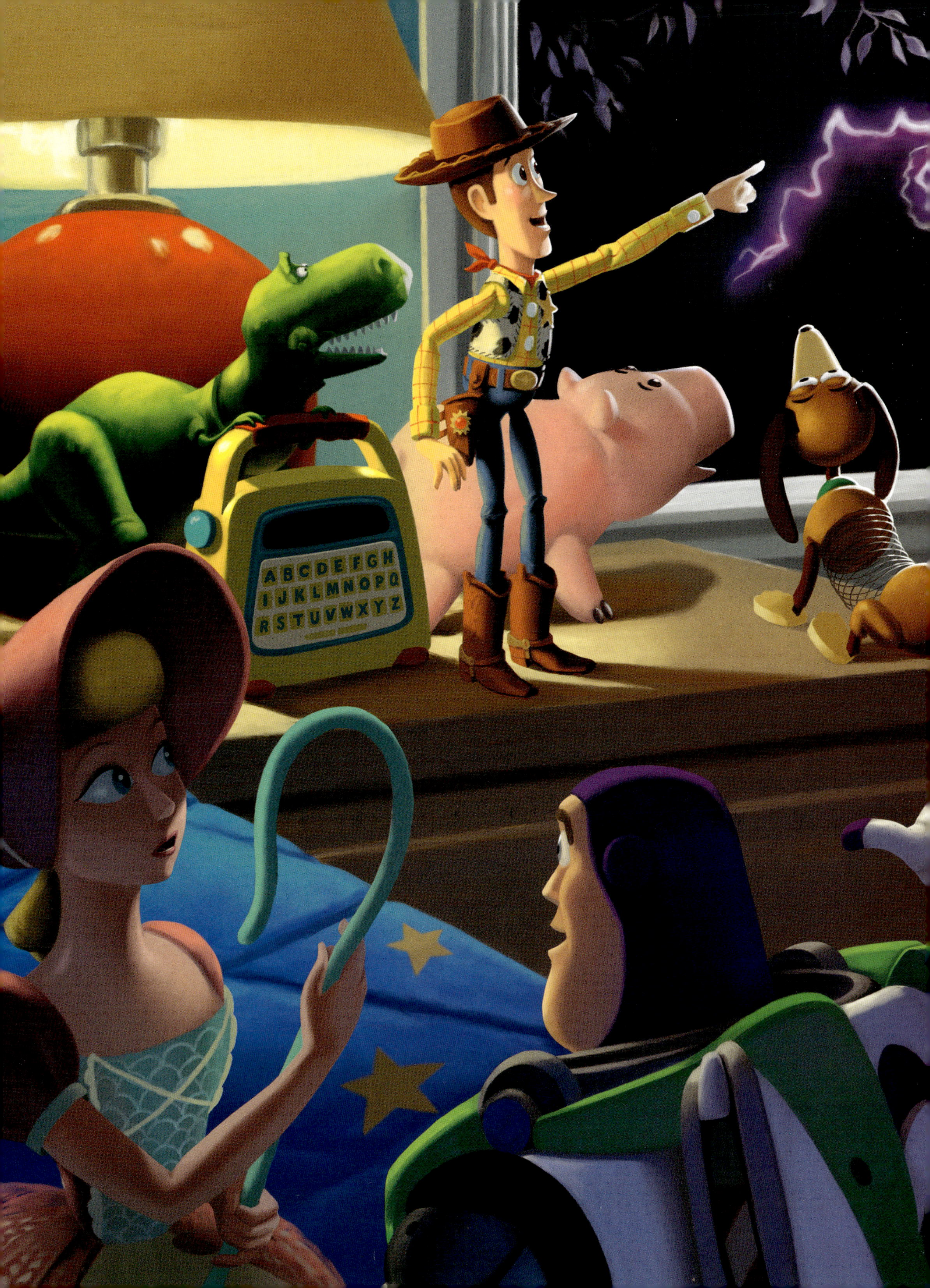
ABCDEFGH
IJKLMNOPQ
RSTUVWXYZ

'Okay, then,' said Woody, 'scary stories it is. Gather around, everybody.'

'There I am, trapped on a planet filled with six-headed aliens,' continued Buzz. 'The creatures close in on me. They are ready to blast me with their laser guns. But at the last minute, I activate my jet pack and blast straight up into the sky. Instead of hitting me, the rays from the aliens' guns bounce back off the rocks and stun my attackers while I make a clean getaway.'

'Ohhhh!' said the Little Green Aliens.

'Sorry, fellas,' said Buzz. 'Besides, the aliens in the video game are evil, not nice guys like you three.'

'May I go next?' asked Rex.

Rex's story was about the most ferocious dinosaur on Earth. 'He had enormous pointy teeth and a fierce roar,' Rex said. Then he roared himself. No-one jumped or screamed.

'Did I scare you?' Rex asked his friends.

'Sure,' Woody replied. He winked at the other toys. All the toys knew Rex was the *least* ferocious dinosaur around. But they didn't want to hurt his feelings.

Rex told the other toys about the creature's bad breath, big eyes and super-sharp claws. 'His jaws were like a steel trap!' Rex exclaimed. 'He could crush dinosaurs twice his size!' Then Rex shivered with fright.

Woody volunteered to tell the next scary story.

'Did I ever tell you guys about the time Andy and I went to a haunted house?' he asked.

The toys all shook their heads. 'Well, there we were, walking by a house that was all decorated. Suddenly, these ghosts rose up out of the lawn! Andy ran for the front porch and rang the bell. But a vampire answered the door and he was holding a black cat that had bright yellow eyes.'

'W-w-w-what happened next?' Rex asked.

'Then a monster chased us back down to the footpath,' Woody answered.

He noticed that the other toys looked afraid. Bo had clutched Woody's arm and Hamm was shaking so much that his coins were clinking.

'Don't worry, guys. Andy's brave. And I'm here to tell the tale!' Woody said. 'It was all fake!'

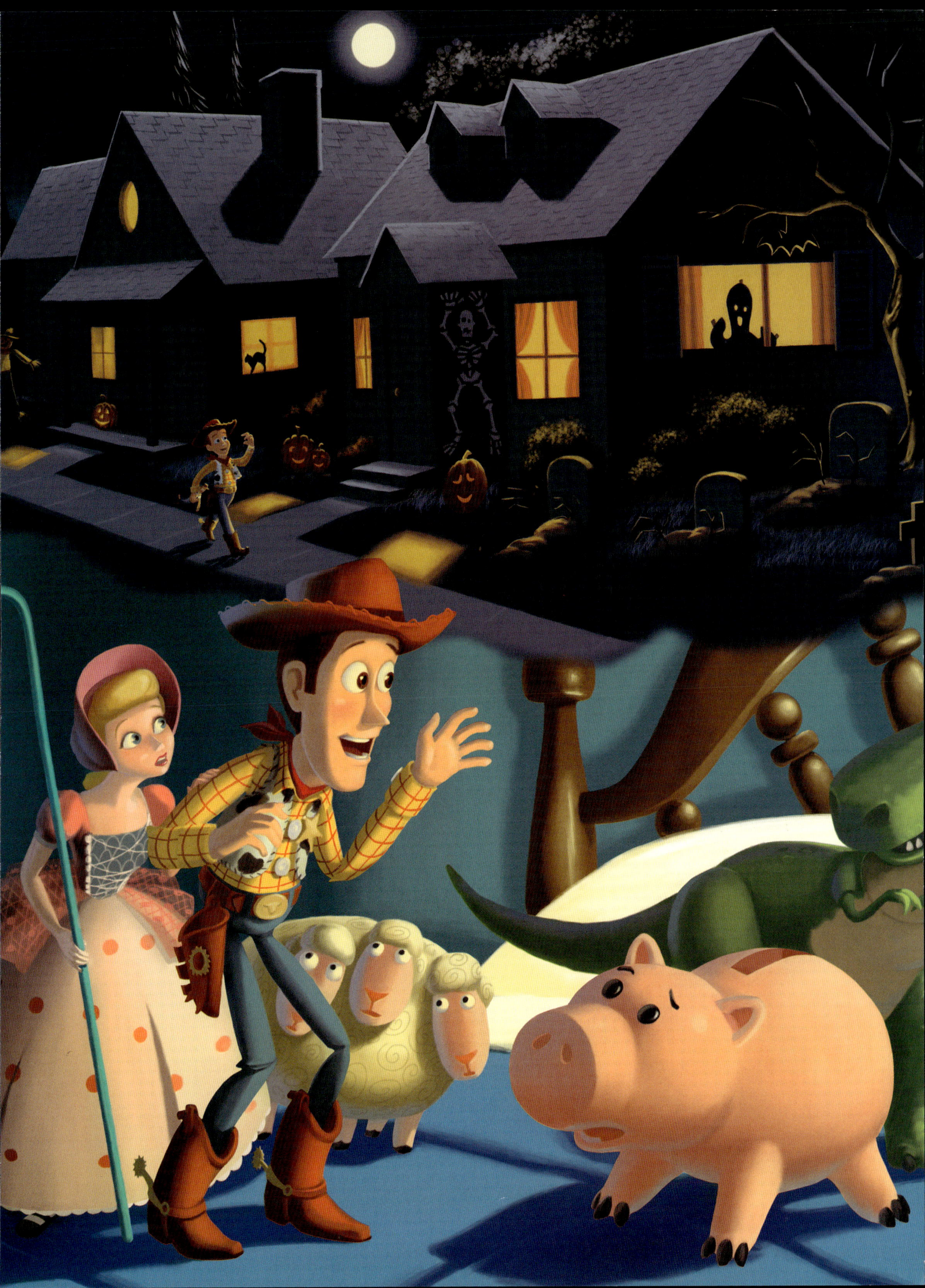

'I knew that,' said Rex. But Woody could see that his arms were still trembling.

'The people who owned the house set everything up to scare the trick-or-treaters,' Woody said. He rubbed his chin. 'Maybe that one was a little too scary.'

'All right, gang,' Woody continued, 'I think we've had enough stories for tonight. Let's get some sleep. Andy will be home bright and early tomorrow morning.'

Woody had just fallen asleep when he felt a nudge. He moved over a little, but then he felt another small shove.

'Woody! Woody!' Rex whispered.

'Huh?' Woody said groggily. 'What is it?'

'I heard something,' said Rex. 'It's coming from under Andy's bed.'

'You must have been dreaming,' Woody replied.

'I know I wasn't dreaming, because I haven't gone to sleep yet,' Rex explained.

'Maybe it was a noise from the storm,' Woody said.

'The storm is over,' said Rex.

'You're going to make me get up and check, aren't you?' asked Woody.

'If it wouldn't be too much trouble,' Rex answered.

'All right,' said Woody. 'Let's go have a look under the bed. You'll see there's nothing to worry about.'

When they reached the side of the bed, Woody lifted the bedspread. 'It's too dark to see anything under there,' he said. 'But everything seems okay to me.'

GRRRRRR!

'Good job, Rex,' Woody added. 'If there was anything around here, I'm sure you just scared it off.'

'That wasn't me,' Rex said, his voice shaky.

'It wasn't?' asked Woody.

Something went BUMP underneath the bed.

'Looks like you did hear something, after all,' Woody admitted. He was starting to feel a little nervous, too. 'Let's go get Buzz before we do any more investigating.'

'This had better be an emergency,' Buzz declared when Woody woke him.

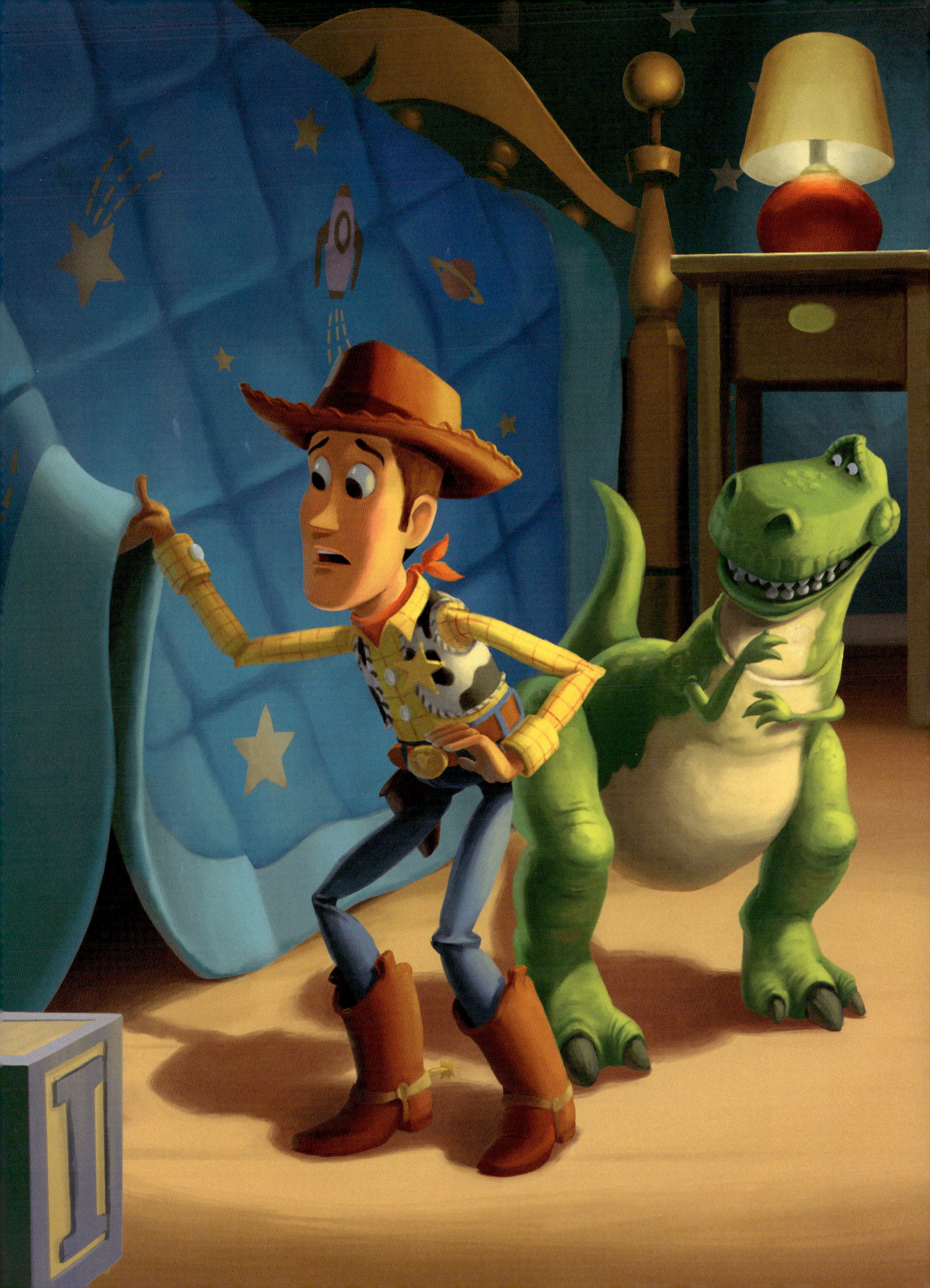

'I think we have an intruder,' Woody whispered.

'What's going on?' asked Hamm.

'It's nothing to worry about,' said Woody as calmly as he could. 'There appears to be something—or someone—under Andy's bed.'

At that moment, a rumbling came from under the bed.

'It sounds hungry!' Rex wailed and then fainted from the fright.

The toys crept out of their places in drawers, behind furniture and in the toy box. They gathered in the centre of the room while Woody woke Rex.

Buzz strode confidently up to the bed. 'This is Buzz Lightyear, space ranger. You are in violation of Intergalactic Code 36920-Q, which clearly prohibits concealing oneself under another life-form's sleeping unit without prior clearance. It's bad manners. Not to mention creepy. Reveal yourself.'

The only response was a high-pitched whine.

'Very well, then,' Buzz replied. 'You leave me no choice but to take you captive.'

Buzz began to crawl under the bed. Suddenly, his space wings shot out and caught on the bedspread.

'I need some help here,' Buzz called out. He wriggled around but he couldn't free himself.

'Oh, no!' cried Rex, panicking. 'It's got Buzz!'

'Come on, men! We're going in!' cried Sarge. He and the Green Army Men rushed under the bed. They freed Buzz and pulled him back out.

'There's something under there,' Buzz replied. 'And it was definitely moving.'

'We'll take over from here,' Sarge announced. 'Men, we're going to execute a sneak attack and surround the enemy. You know what to do. Now go, go, go!'

The soldiers split into groups and stormed under the bed.

'Halt!' boomed Sarge's voice. 'It's one of our own! Switch to rescue-mission protocol!'

The other toys all looked at each other. 'What's going on?' called Woody. 'Who is it?'

But there was no answer. All the toys heard was the soldiers moving around under the bed.

'Push, men! Push!' commanded Sarge. 'Now, one . . . two . . . three . . . heave-ho!'

Suddenly, RC Car shot out into the room.

'What was he doing under there?' asked Woody.

'His batteries are nearly out of juice,' Sarge reported. 'He just sat there revving his engine, spinning his wheels and going nowhere.'

'I knew there had to be a reasonable explanation,' said Rex.

Woody smiled and patted his friend on the back. 'You're right, buddy,' he said.

Meanwhile, Buzz had removed RC's battery door.

'The supply truck's coming,' Sarge told Buzz. 'Let's go, men!' he commanded his soldiers.

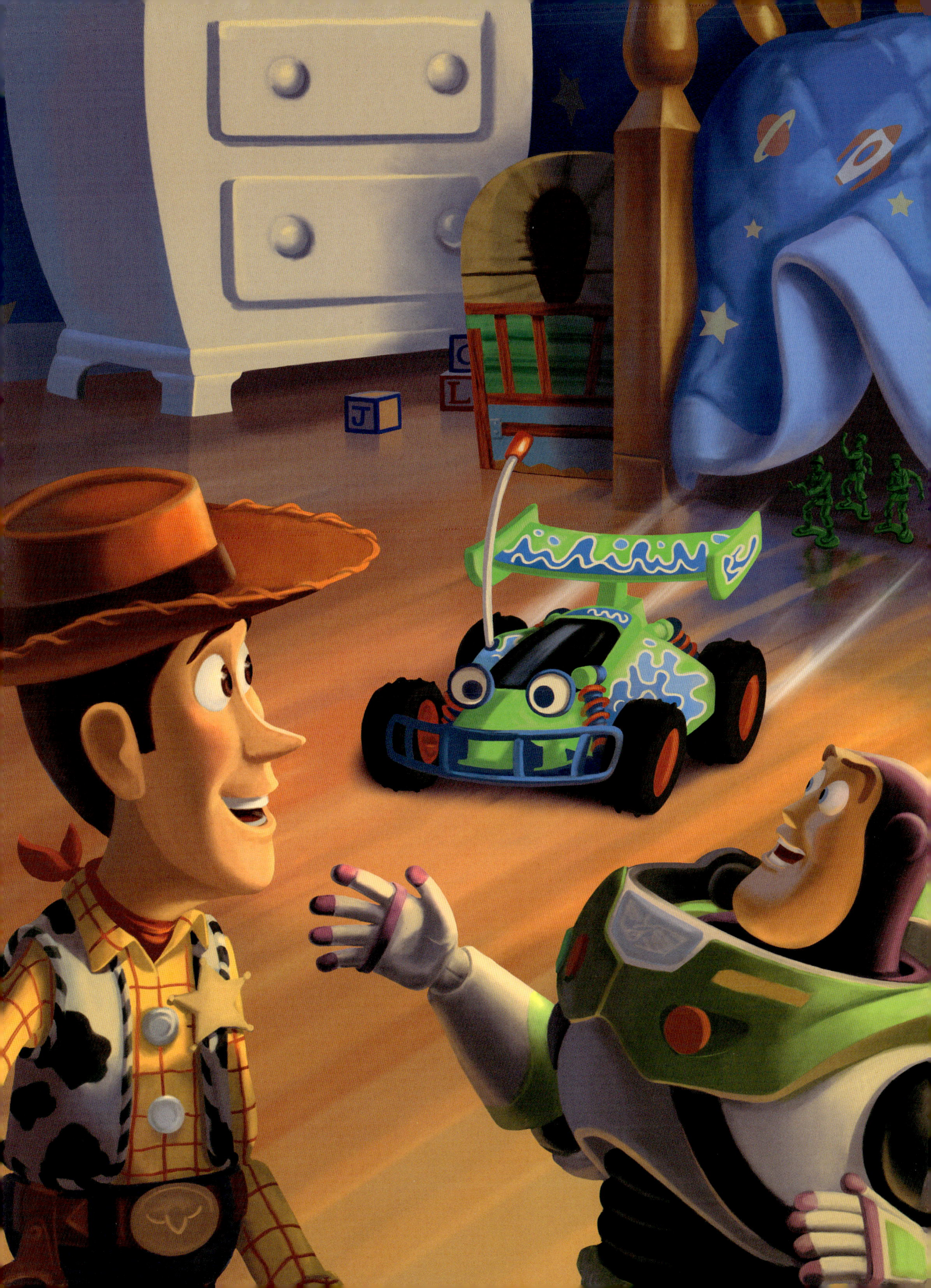

Soon, RC was zipping around the room, good as new.

'Don't we feel silly?' said Hamm. 'All of us so afraid, and it was only RC.'

Just then, Mr Spell lit up. 'A low battery is scary!' he said. 'In fact, I am feeling . . . a . . . bit . . . sluggish . . . myself.'

'Make a note, Slinky,' said Woody. 'Tomorrow, fresh double-A's all around!'

Disney · PIXAR
TOY STORY
Rocket Launchers

Woody the cowboy doll stood at the window in Andy's bedroom, peeking outside at the school bus. He heard the front door slam downstairs. Then he saw Andy run down the driveway, his backpack bouncing behind him.

Andy stepped onto the school bus, and the bus quickly pulled away.

Woody watched until the bus turned the corner and was out of sight. Then he turned around and looked at the other toys in Andy's room. 'All clear!' he announced. 'Andy's off to school.'

The toys gathered on the floor in the middle of the room, surrounding a long cardboard box. Andy had brought it home the night before. Woody climbed down from the desk and walked over to the box. 'Now,' Woody said, 'let's get a look at whatever this is.'

Woody flipped open the box flaps and looked inside. He saw several rubber tubes and a tall plastic stand.

'What's in there?' Slinky Dog asked. He nudged Woody and looked inside.

'I'm not sure, Slink,' Woody said. He pulled a piece of paper out of the box. After a couple of minutes he smiled. 'It's a rocket launcher,' he said.

'How far do you think it goes?' Rex the dinosaur asked.

'There's only one way to find out,' Buzz Lightyear the space ranger replied. He started to lift pieces out of the box.

Woody helped Buzz put the rocket together. When it was finished, Buzz said, 'Now, who wants to go first?'

'I do!' Jessie said as she jumped up and raised her hand.

Buzz showed her what to do. There was a pump attached to the launch pad. Jessie stepped on the pump as hard as she could, and the rocket shot up into the air. It floated for a minute before landing lightly on Andy's desk.

'Cool,' said Hamm, the piggy bank. 'Can I try?'

'Sure, everyone can try,' Woody said. He climbed up onto the desk and pushed the rocket off.

When it was all set up again, Hamm stomped on the pump. *Whoosh!* The rocket shot all the way across the room.

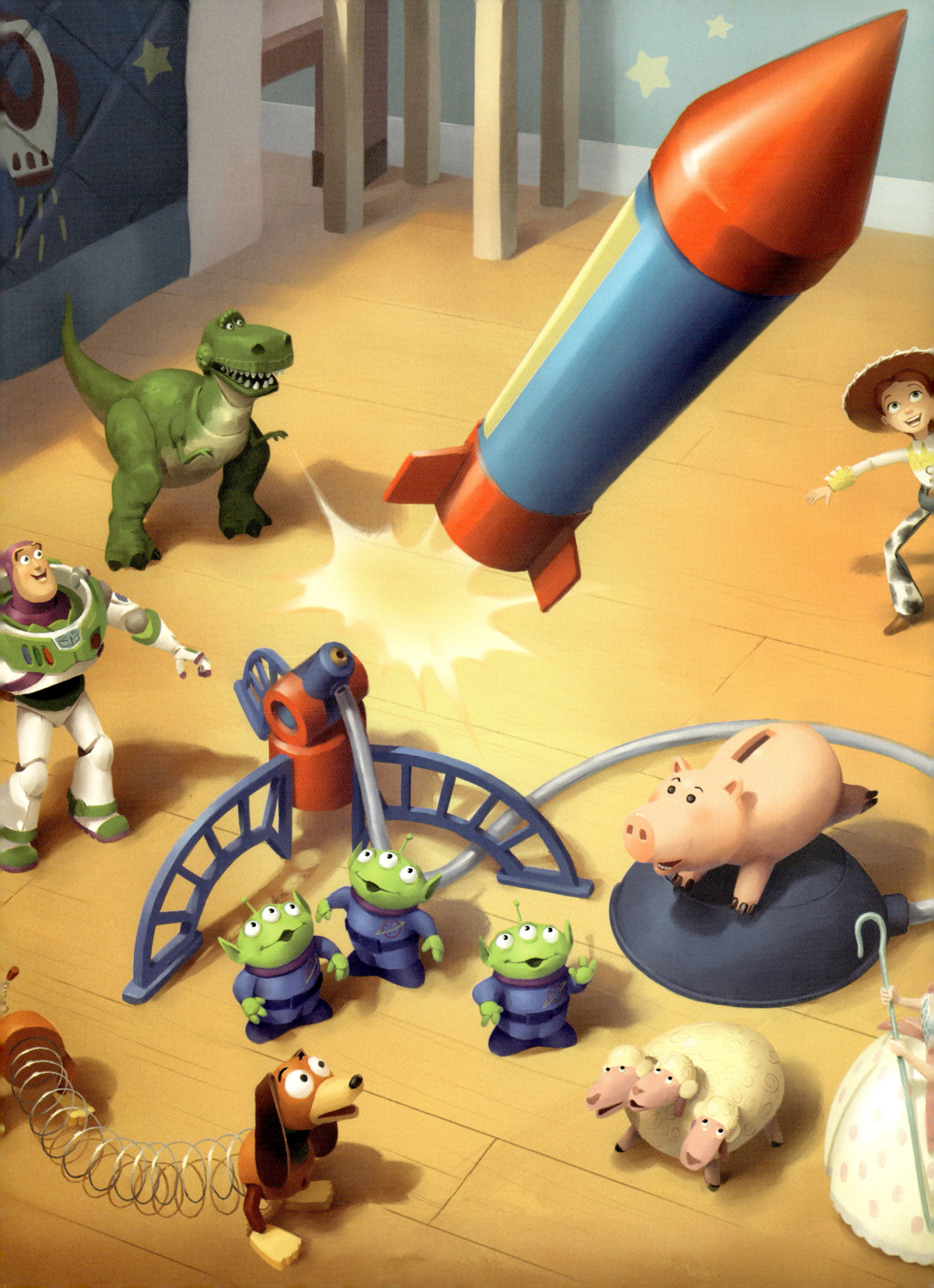

'Look at that,' said Rex. 'The harder you stomp, the further it goes.'

Soon, all the toys wanted to see how far each of them could make the rocket fly.

Buzz and Woody helped set up the rocket for each toy and then measured the distance the rocket flew with the string from a yo-yo. Some toys launched the rocket straight up in the air, while others aimed for the desktop or the door to Andy's room.

'Looks like we have a tie,' said Buzz after all the toys had taken a turn.

'Yep,' Woody agreed. 'Hamm and Slink both made it all the way to Andy's door.'

'We need a tie breaker!' Jessie said.

'That's a great idea,' Woody replied. He helped Buzz set up the rocket, then they turned to face the other toys.

'What about best out of three?' Rex offered.

'That'll take too long,' Jessie said. She was eager to see who the winner would be.

'We could do one final stomp,' Buzz suggested. 'That puts the pressure on Slink and Hamm.'

'That's okay,' said Slinky Dog.

'Yeah,' agreed Hamm. 'One more stomp sounds good to me.'

Woody held his hands behind his back. Slinky Dog and Hamm had to guess how many fingers he was holding up to see who would go first. Slinky picked five and Hamm guessed three.

'Five is right! Slinky goes first,' Woody said, holding up his wide-open hand.

Slinky Dog walked over to the rocket. He stretched his body and rolled his head from side to side to loosen up. When he was ready, he nodded to Buzz.

'Okay,' Buzz announced to all the toys. 'This is it, the big stomp. Slinky and Hamm will each try to launch the rocket as far as they can by stomping on the pump. They only get one try. Whoever's rocket flies the furthest is the winner.'

The other toys fell silent as they watched Slinky Dog step up to the pump. Slinky lifted his front paw. *'Grr,'* he said as he pushed down on the pump as hard as he could. The rocket didn't move.

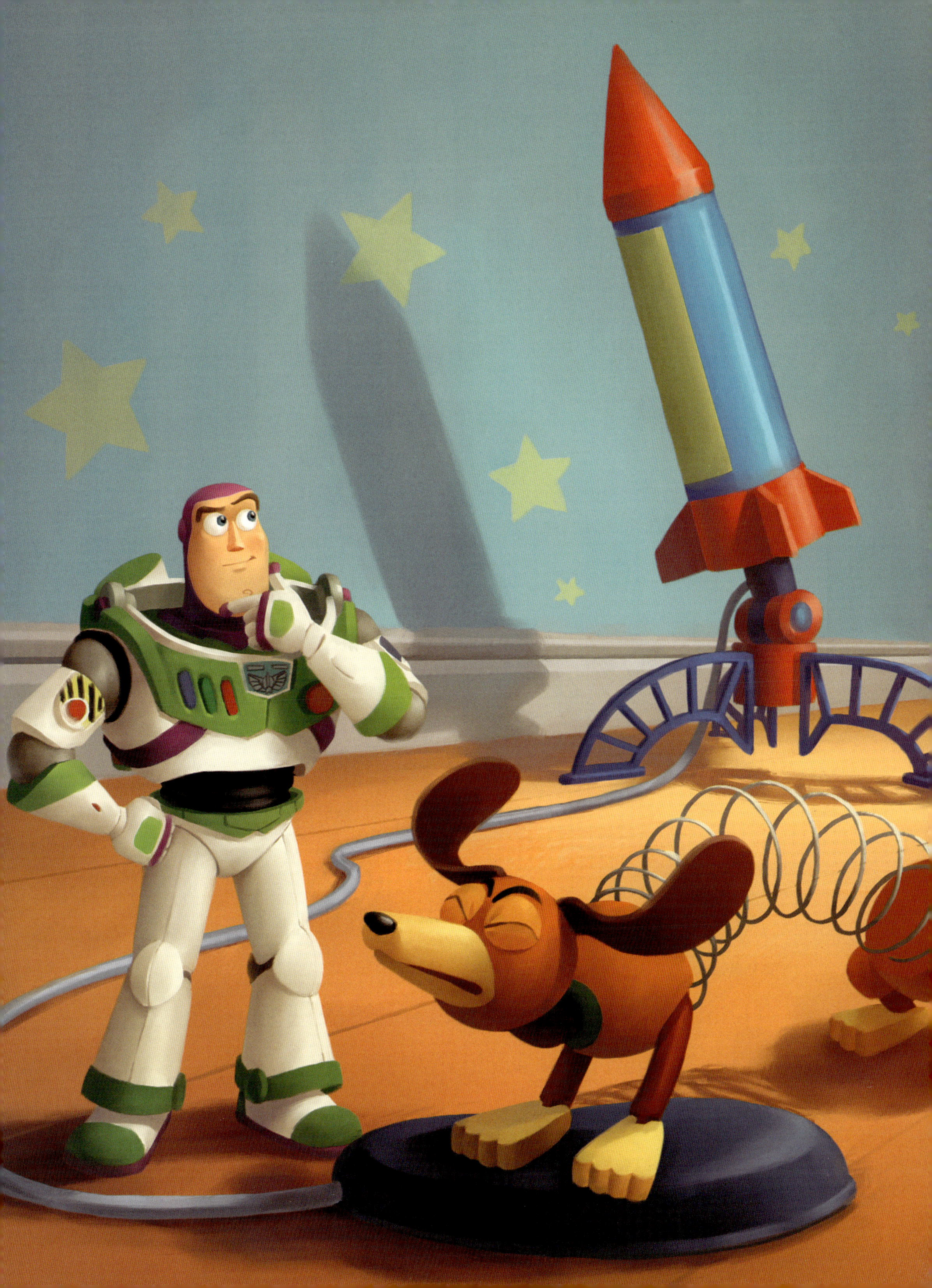

Slinky Dog looked at the rocket sitting on its stand. 'What happened?' he asked.

'I don't know, Slink,' Buzz said as he walked around the rocket. 'It looks like it's all set up correctly. I don't know why it didn't move.'

'Maybe Slinky should try again,' Rex suggested.

'Or Hamm could go,' Jessie said.

Hamm walked up to the rocket as Slinky Dog backed away. 'I'll give it a try,' he said.

He counted to three and then stomped his foot on the pump. But the rocket still didn't move.

'Well, now we know something's wrong if no-one can make it move,' Woody said as he walked up to the rocket. He looked at Buzz. 'What do you think happened?'

Buzz smiled. 'I think we have some space invaders,' he said. He walked around the side of the rocket and opened a small door.

The three Little Green Aliens peered out at Buzz and the rest of the toys.

'Hey, guys,' Woody said. 'What are you doing in there?'

'Go to Earth,' the aliens said together. One of them pointed towards the corner of the room by Andy's desk.

Woody looked at Buzz, confused. Buzz looked over at the desk and saw a globe sitting on top. Andy had been using it the night before for a school project.

Buzz helped the aliens climb out of the rocket. 'Sorry, guys,' he said. 'You're already on Earth. That is just a tiny scale model of the real—'

'Um, Buzz,' Woody interrupted. He knew Buzz could ramble on about the galaxy for hours. 'Can we get back to the contest? Slinky and Hamm want to see who can shoot this rocket to the moon!'

The other toys clapped and cheered, ready to get the contest back underway. Slinky Dog stretched again as he waited for Buzz to give him the all-clear. Then he stepped up to the pump.

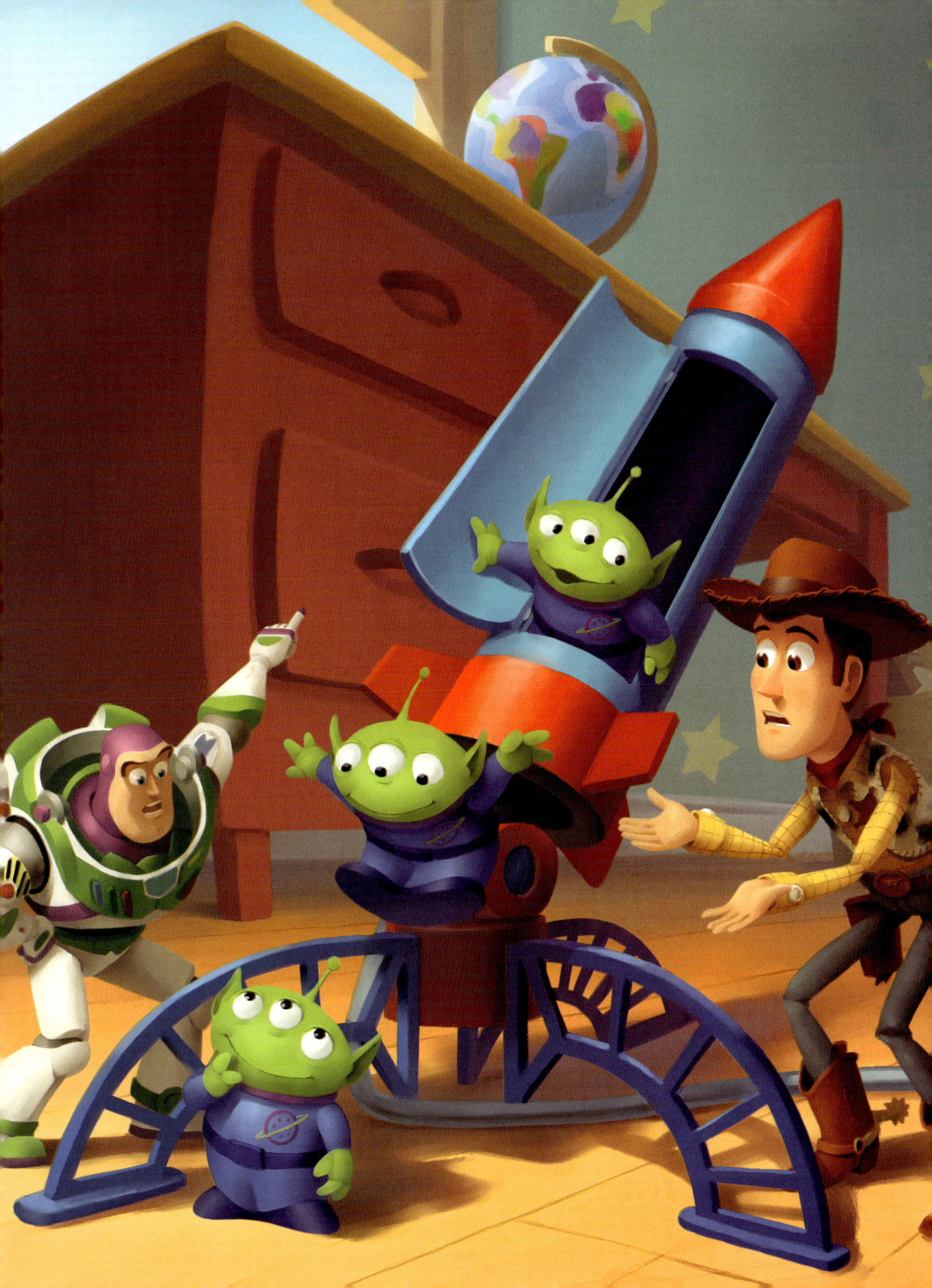

Slinky Dog stomped on the pump as hard as he could. The rocket shot off the stand and flew across the room.

'Oooh,' the Little Green Aliens said as they watched it fly.

'Good job, Slink!' Woody said.

'That'll be a tough one to beat,' said Rex, who had scurried across the room after the rocket. He waited by it while Woody measured the distance with the string.

Hamm stepped up for his turn. Rex was waiting across the room, where Slinky Dog's rocket had landed, to show Hamm how far his had to go. Hamm stomped on the pump and his rocket shot into the air. Everyone held their breath as they watched it fly. Then it landed . . . in the same place Slinky Dog's had!

'Another tie!' Jessie yelled. 'What do we do now?'

Slinky Dog looked at Hamm. Hamm looked at Slinky. 'What if we give the aliens a ride?' Hamm suggested.

'That's a great idea!' Woody exclaimed as the aliens cheered.

'Ride into space,' they said as they shuffled back over to the launching pad.

'You'll have to go one at a time,' Buzz said as he helped the first alien into the rocket. He stuck a handkerchief into the small space around the alien. 'Can't hurt to have some extra cushioning,' he said.

For the rest of the morning, the aliens rode one at a time in the rocket. Each of the toys took a turn stomping on the pump to see how far they could make the aliens fly.

When the other toys got tired of playing with the rocket, Buzz and the aliens sat beside the globe.

'Well, fellas,' Buzz said, 'what did you think about your rocket ride?'

'Fun,' they said. 'Tomorrow we go home.'

'You *are* home, guys,' he said.

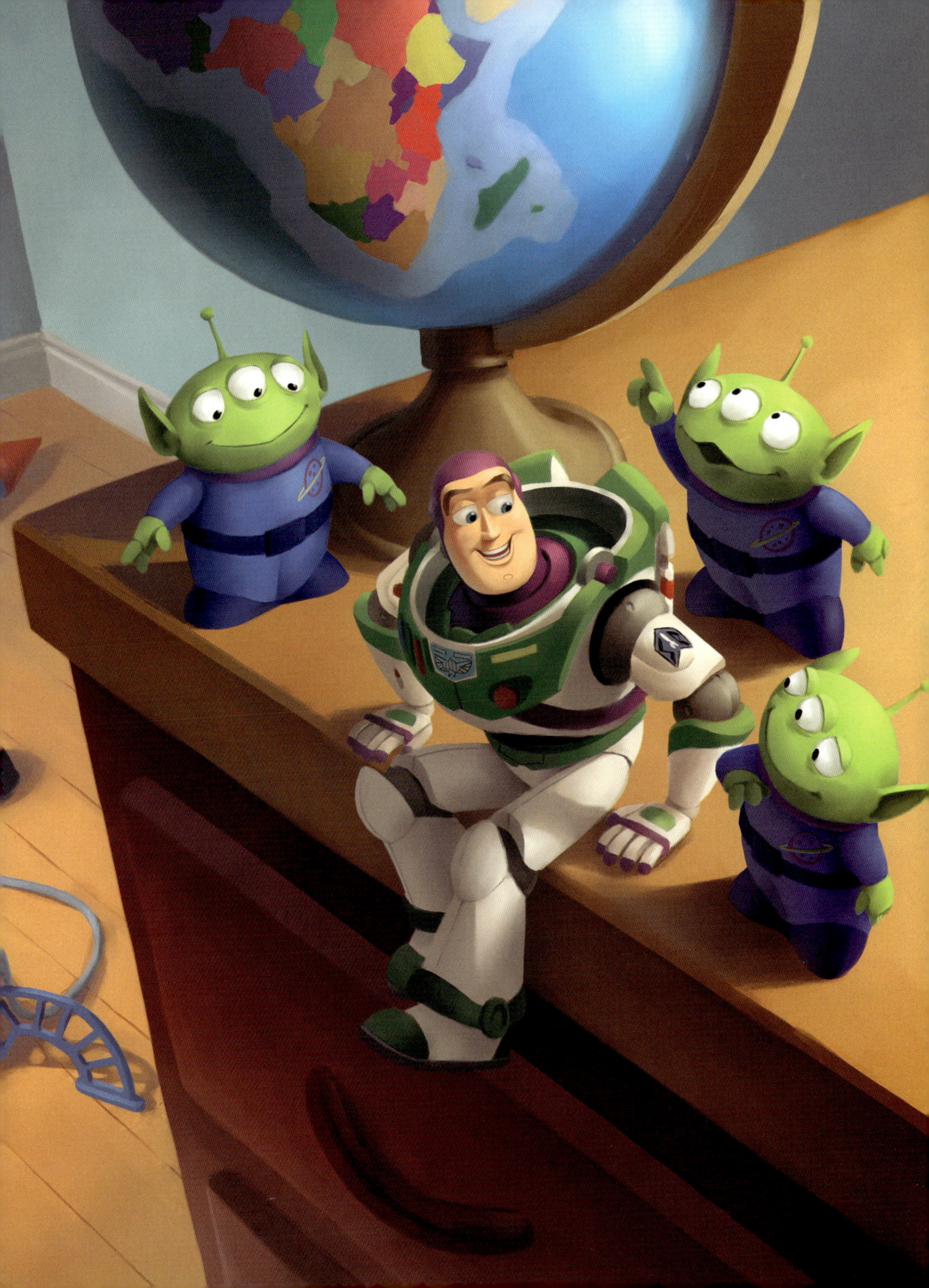

'How are our space invaders doing?' Woody asked as he walked over. 'Slinky and Hamm were just saying that they think if they worked together they could launch all three of you in one go.'

'Oooooh,' the aliens said.

Buzz stood up and gave Andy's globe a spin. 'There's a plan,' he said. 'Teamwork will get us out of the galaxy, to the moon—'

'To infinity and beyond!' Woody finished.

Disney · Pixar
TOY STORY

Woody's Quest for a Date

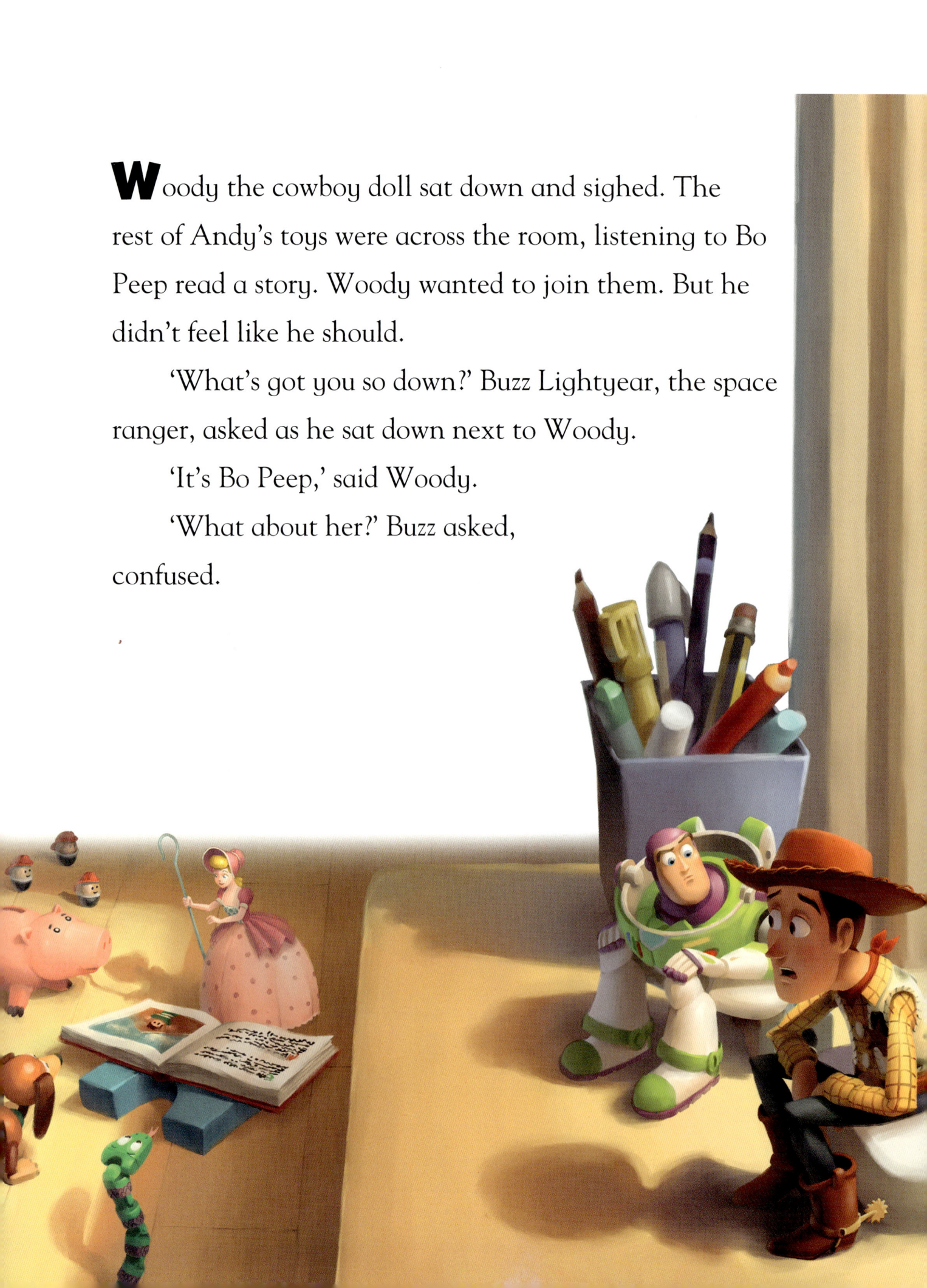

Woody the cowboy doll sat down and sighed. The rest of Andy's toys were across the room, listening to Bo Peep read a story. Woody wanted to join them. But he didn't feel like he should.

'What's got you so down?' Buzz Lightyear, the space ranger, asked as he sat down next to Woody.

'It's Bo Peep,' said Woody.

'What about her?' Buzz asked, confused.

'I don't know,' Woody said. He shrugged. 'I've been thinking lately that I need to do something to impress her.'

'Hmm . . . something to impress a lady?' Buzz rubbed his chin. 'When was the last time you saw Bo excited by anything?'

Woody looked at Buzz and smiled. 'When you showed us all how you could fly,' he said. 'Buzz, do you think you could teach me?'

'Of course!' Buzz said. 'To Bo's heart and beyond!'

Before they started to practise, Buzz warned Woody that flying could be dangerous. 'You must always be alert,' Buzz told his friend. 'The wind can shift and push you off course. Or if your wings get caught—'

'Buzz,' Woody interrupted. 'Can we get on with the actual flying?' He didn't want to waste another second.

'Yeah, let's get this show in the air,' Rex the dinosaur said. He'd come over to watch, along with Hamm the piggy bank and Slinky Dog.

'Okay then,' Buzz said. 'Strap on your wings.'

He helped Woody put on the wings they'd made out of paper. The paper was glued to some rubber bands.

Woody looked back at the wings. He started to wonder if they were sturdy enough to help him fly. But before he could say anything, he was pushed forwards.

'Time to take flight!' Buzz called.

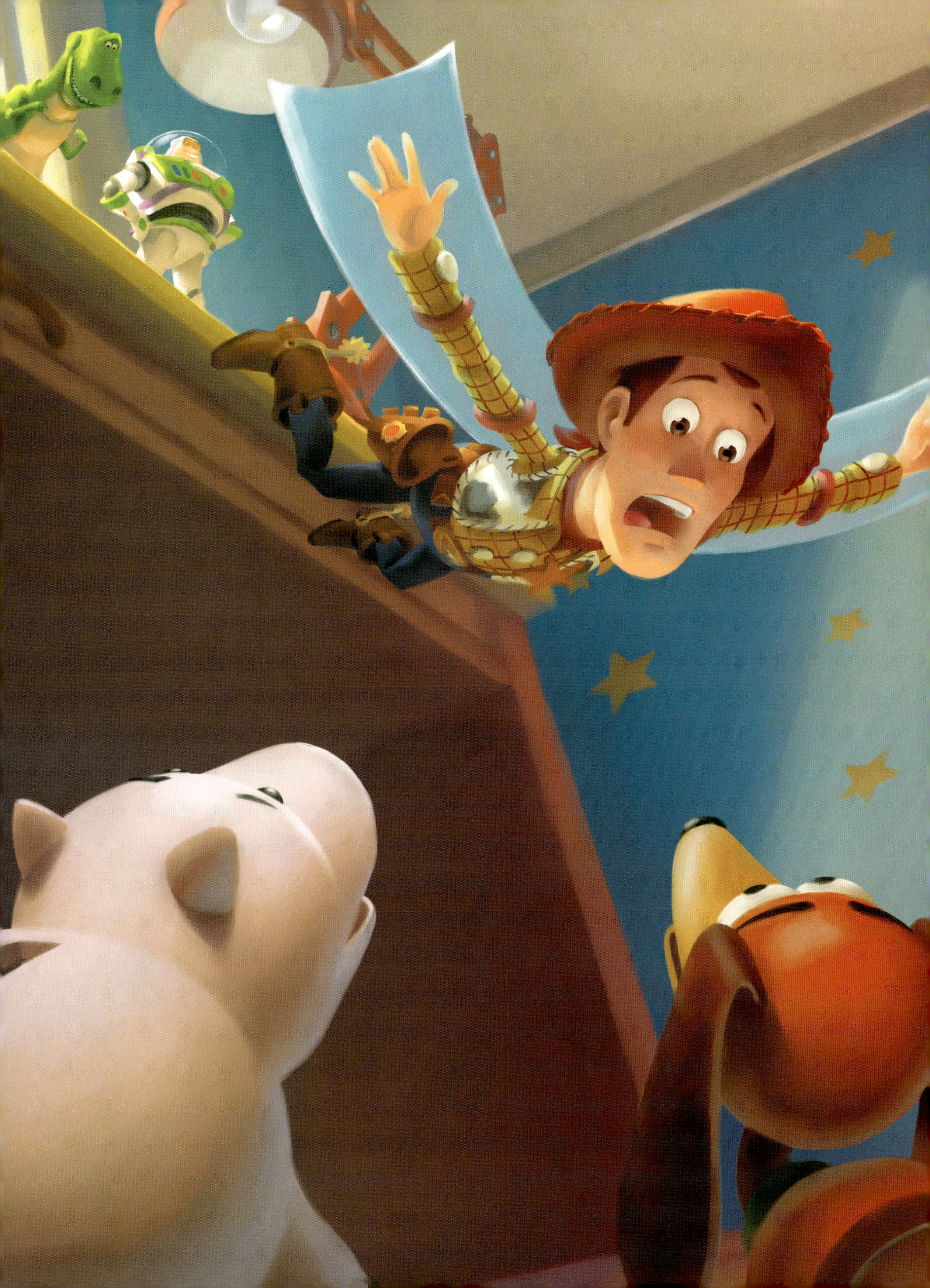

Woody landed on the floor with a thud. 'Ouch,' he said as he stood up. He rubbed his elbow.

'Hmm, maybe we need to practice some more,' Buzz called from up on the desk.

Woody took off his wings. The paper was crumpled and torn. 'I think we better come up with a new idea,' Woody said.

Later that day, Sarge and the Green Army Men tried to help Woody.

'You know what you need, soldier,' Sarge said. 'Some basic training. The first thing you need to do is bulk up.'

'Umm . . . okay,' Woody said. 'If you think it will impress Bo.'

'Excuse me?' Sarge barked.

'I mean, sir, yes, sir!' Woody shouted, standing at attention.

'Let's get started!' Sarge said. 'Climb that rope, soldier! Go, go, go!'

Woody tried to climb a long cord that was hanging from the curtains. But he didn't make it very far. 'Sarge,' Woody called as he dangled above the floor. 'Are you sure this is the way to impress Bo?'

Sarge was sure. He made Woody lift barbells and run through an obstacle course. He had him do push-ups and chin-ups and sit-ups.

Woody was exhausted. But he perked up when he saw the perfect opportunity to show Bo his new strength.

Bo was trying to get a book off a shelf, but it was wedged in so tightly that it wouldn't budge.

Woody hurried over to help her. 'Allow me,' he said.

He pulled the book with all his might, but nothing happened. He pulled again and again but still the book wouldn't move.

Woody felt terrible. All his training had made him too tired to lift a book.

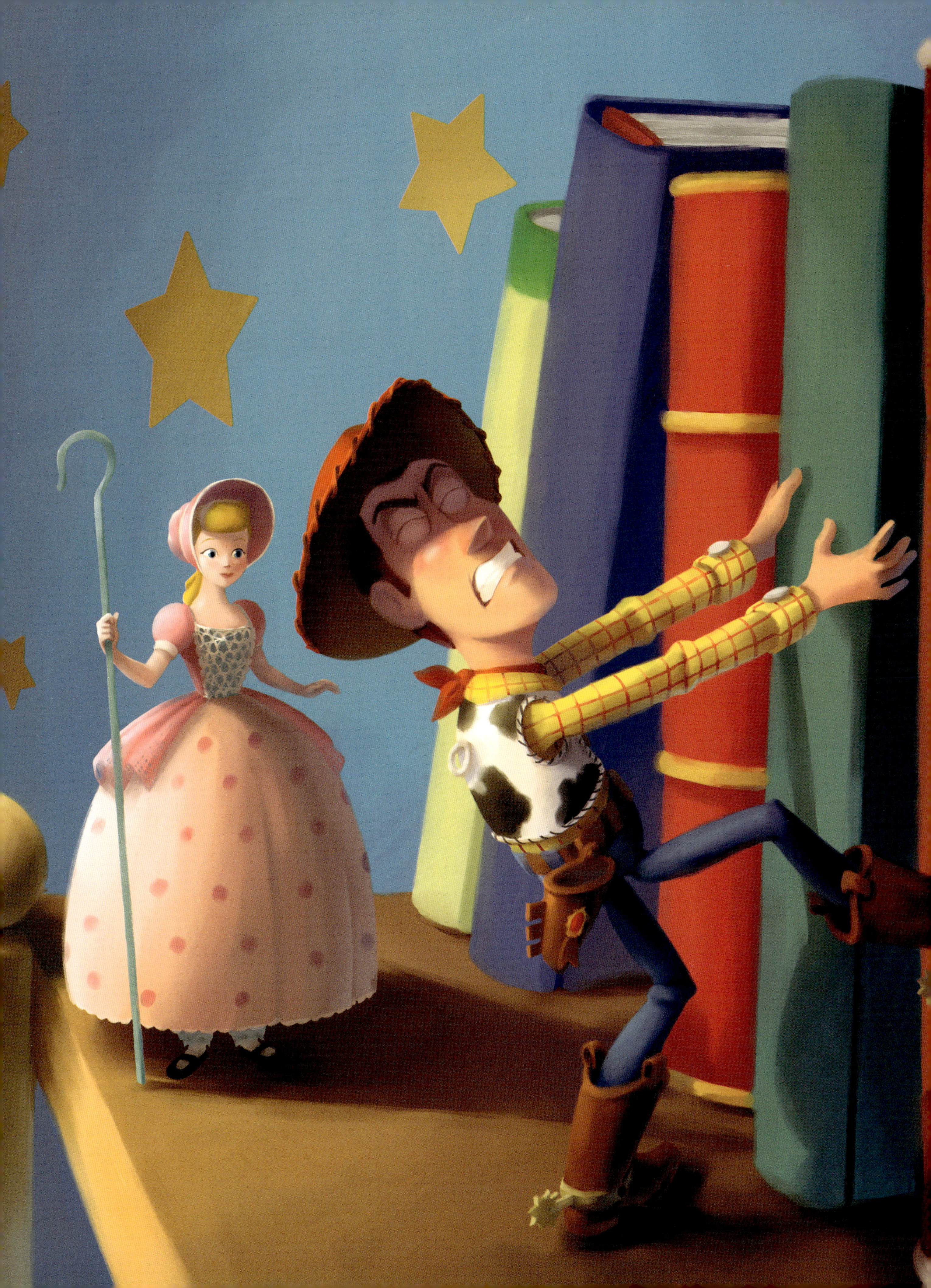

While the Little Green Aliens helped Bo with her book, Woody walked over to the bed. After his workout and flying lesson, he needed a nap.

Wheezy the penguin danced over to Woody. He was singing a cheerful tune.

Woody couldn't help but smile. Then he had an idea. 'Hey, Wheezy,' he said. 'Do you think you could teach me how to sing like that? I'll bet Bo would really get a kick out of it.'

'No problem,' Wheezy replied. 'Let's hear what you've got.'

'La, la, la, la, la,' screeched Woody.

Wheezy winced. 'Not to worry,' he reassured Woody. 'I've got an idea.'

That night, Woody gave Bo her very own concert. She sat down with her sheep to watch.

Woody began to 'sing' a romantic song—but Bo couldn't help noticing that his voice seemed to be coming from somewhere else.

Bo got up, went over to the curtain and pulled it aside. There was Wheezy, singing away while Woody pretended it was his voice.

'Very funny, you two,' Bo said. Then she walked away.

Woody didn't know what to try next. He thought that maybe he needed a girl's opinion. The next morning, he decided to ask Jessie what she thought.

'What a gal likes is a guy who's got a lot of enthusiasm!' Jessie said. 'Maybe you need to pick up the pace instead of moseyin' around all the time. Really show her you're interested, you know what I mean?'

'Maybe,' said Woody. But he wasn't so sure.

'Don't be shy now,' Jessie coached him. 'Go lasso that pretty little gal of yours before someone else does!'

The next time Woody saw Bo, he tried out his new act. 'Hi, Bo!' he shouted. 'It's a beautiful day, isn't it? That's a lovely dress you're wearing. How are those sheep of yours? You sure do take good care of them!' Then he linked his arm through Bo's and swung her around. 'Yee-ha!' Woody exclaimed. 'Has anyone ever told you that you are a spectacular dancer?'

Bo held onto her bonnet as she spun around. When Woody finally let her go, she looked at him, concerned.

'Woody, I think your string may be wound too tight. Do you want me to take a look at it?'

Woody's face turned red. He didn't want Bo to think there was something wrong with him! He tried to smile and then hurried away.

Later that day, Hamm gave Woody some advice. 'Listen,' Hamm said. 'A lot of ladies like the strong silent type. The less you say, the more she'll want to talk to you.'

'Are you sure?' asked Woody.

'Absolutely,' said Hamm. 'Look, here she comes now!'

Woody nodded. He was ready to try anything.

'Hi, Woody,' said Bo. 'Have you seen my sheep?'

Woody just tipped his hat and smiled.

'Is that a yes or a no?' Bo asked.

When Woody didn't reply again, she shouted, 'Woody! Can you hear me?'

Woody didn't say a word. He adjusted the bandana around his neck.

Bo looked at him, puzzled. Then she walked away.

Woody was starting to wonder if his friends' advice was really any good.

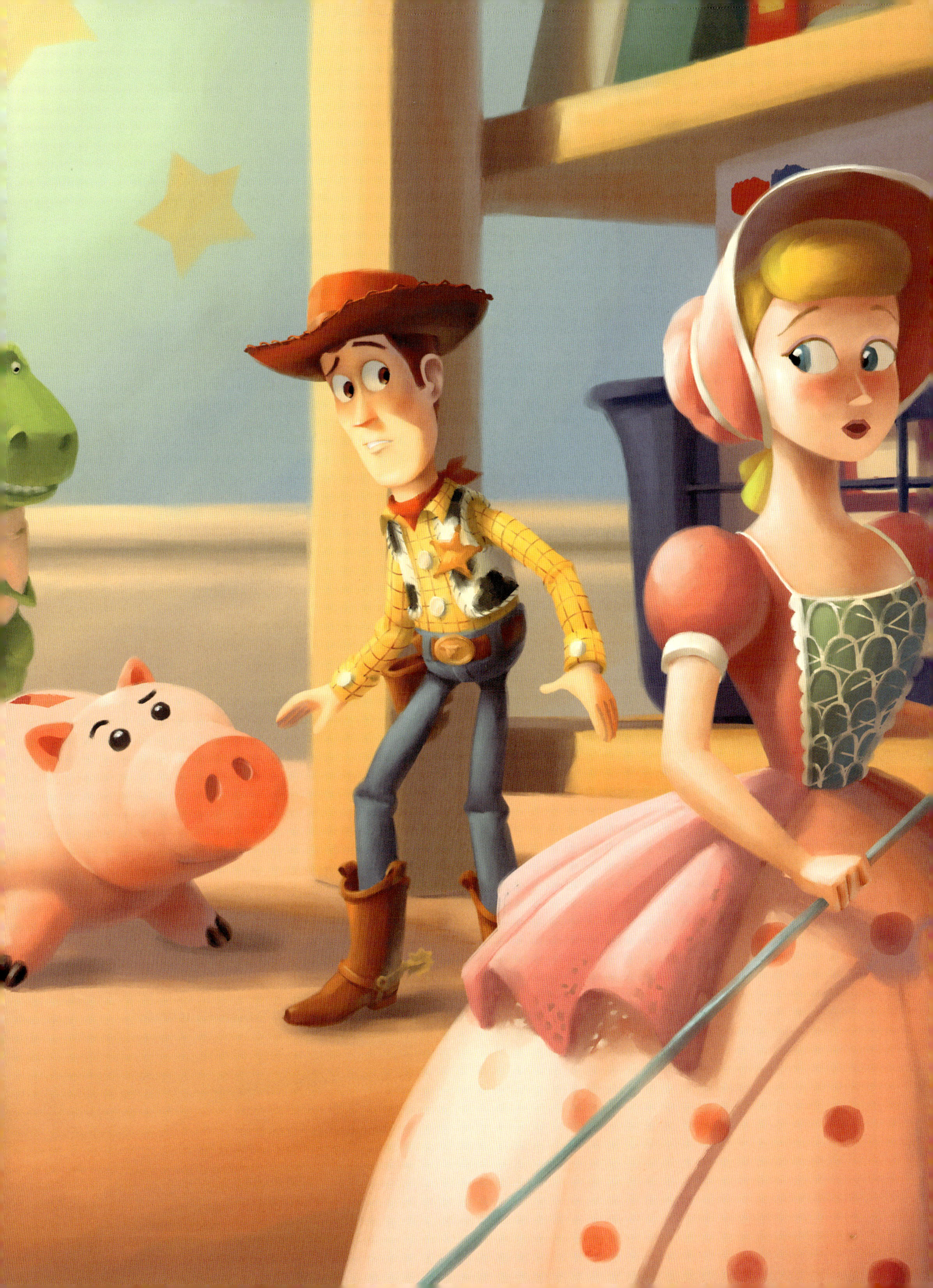

Rex could see his friend was still upset. 'I hope I'm not being too personal here,' he said, 'but why don't you just ask Bo what she's looking for in a man. Then you'll know what impresses her.'

'Rex!' exclaimed Woody. 'That's a brilliant idea!'

'Thank you,' replied Rex. 'It's nice to be known for my brains as well as for my brute strength.'

Woody went straight over to Bo and asked her.

'Well,' Bo answered, 'I like a guy who is kind and smart and funny. Someone who is a good friend. And someone who isn't afraid to be himself.'

'Um . . . have you ever met anyone like that?' Woody asked.

'Oh, Woody!' Bo cried. 'Of course I have! It's you! Although you really haven't been yourself lately.'

'I guess I was trying to get you to like me even more,' Woody admitted.

'Impossible,' said Bo. She planted a kiss on his cheek.

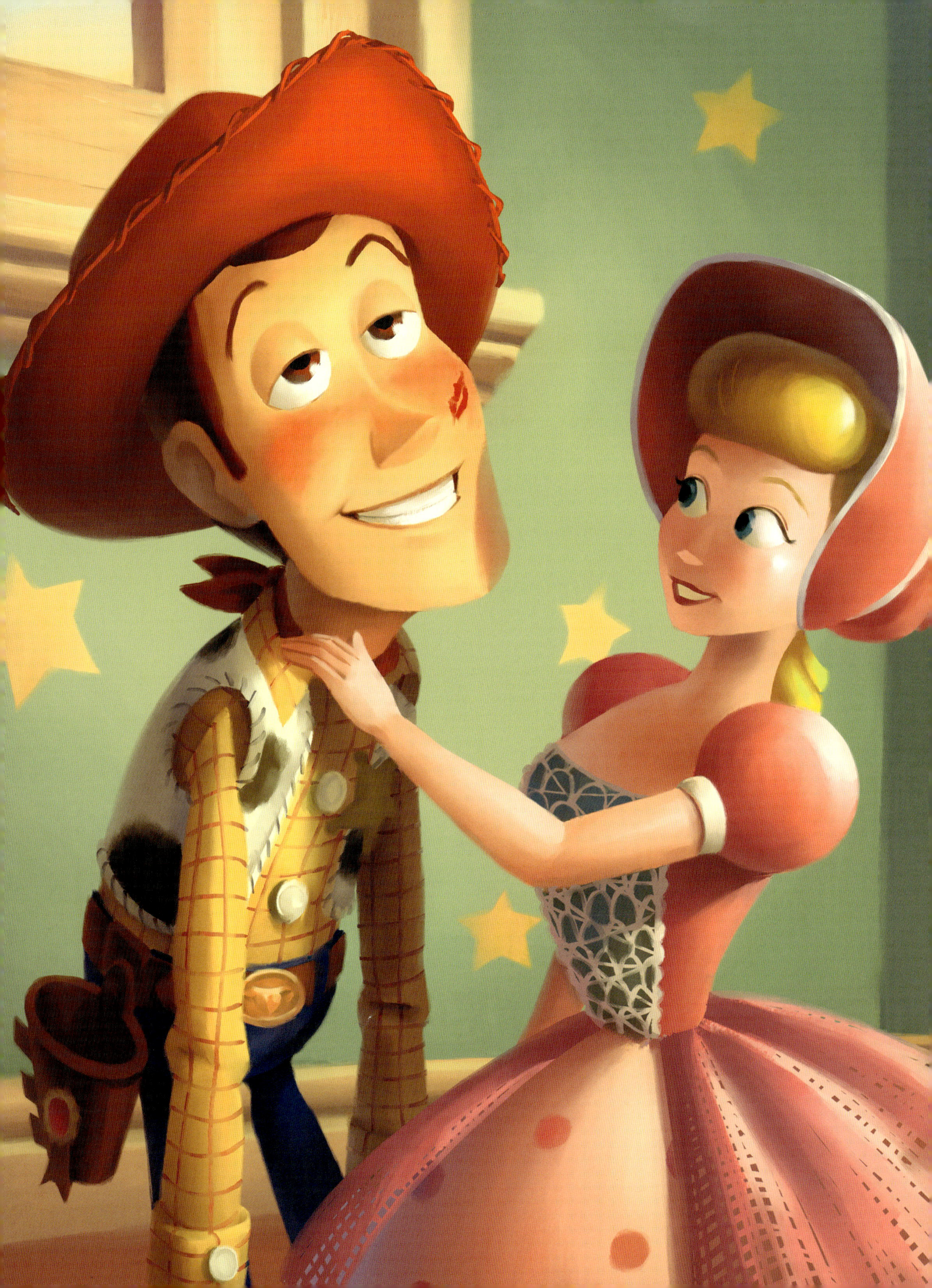

That night, Woody brought Bo a beautiful bouquet of flowers. 'Would you care to join me for a stroll?' he asked.

'I'd be delighted,' answered Bo.

Soon, the pair were talking and laughing and having a wonderful time.

'Now, this is the Woody I've been missing,' said Bo.

'Well, get used to him,' said Woody. ''Cause he's here to stay.'

Bo gave Woody's arm a squeeze. 'I'm glad,' she said, 'because so am I.'

Disney · PIXAR TOY STORY

Toys in Paradise

Andy ran around his room, throwing clothes into a bag. He would be leaving any minute. His best friend's family was going to Florida on holiday and had invited him to come along.

'You're going to have so much fun!' Andy's mother exclaimed as she helped him pack. 'You'll go to the beach and to amusement parks. I wish Molly and I could come along!'

After Andy and his mother left the room, Andy's toys came to life. They gathered on the floor beside Andy's bed where a travel pamphlet lay.

'I'd give anything to go on a tropical holiday,' said Bo Peep. 'Just think of it. The sandy beaches, the blue ocean, the warm sunshine.'

'Not me,' Rex the dinosaur said. 'There are *sharks* in the ocean. And what about *sunburn*?'

'Hey, I've got an idea,' said Jessie the cowgirl. 'Why don't we make our own tropical paradise, right here in Andy's room?'

'We wouldn't even have to fly,' said Rex. He sighed in relief.

'I could use some downtime,' Slinky Dog admitted. 'I've been feeling stretched to my limit lately.'

'Yippee!' Jessie cried. 'What do you think we'll need?'

'This might help,' Woody suggested. The toys gathered around as he flipped open the pamphlet. 'Andy's mum left it behind. This is where Andy is staying.'

'Lounge chairs, umbrellas, water,' Buzz Lightyear the space ranger said. 'We can find all this stuff right here.'

Sarge and the Green Army Men went in search of a potted plant. Hamm and Rex raided the kitchen for Buster's water dish and some sponges. Bo found a doll parasol in Molly's room.

Soon, all the supplies were gathered in the centre of the room.

'Next stop: paradise!' Jessie exclaimed.

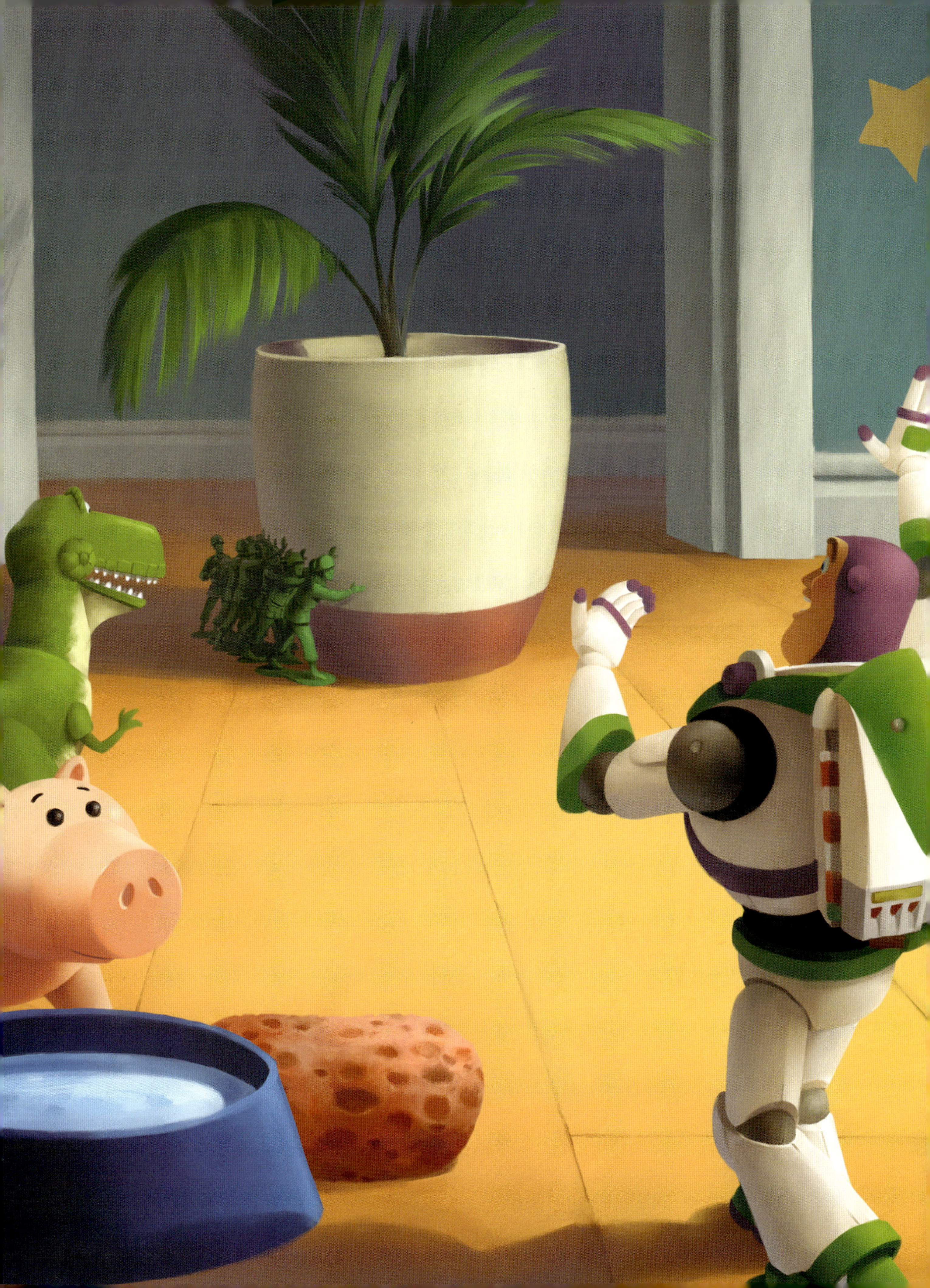

In no time at all, the toys *had* created their own tropical paradise.

'Ahh, this is the life,' Woody said with a sigh. He and Buzz were stretched out on the lounge chairs they had made out of shoebox tops and sponges.

'Wait a minute,' Jessie said. 'We forgot the sun.'

'We can't forget the sun!' exclaimed Buzz. 'Our planet—'

'The *pretend* sun,' Woody reminded him.

'Oh, right,' Buzz replied. 'I know just what we need.' He dragged Andy's desk lamp to the edge of the desk and turned it on. 'Better put on some shades.'

Rex and Hamm were by the makeshift ocean. Hamm looked a little sad. 'What's an ocean without any waves?' he said.

Woody and Buzz hopped off their lounge chairs. They each grabbed a side of the ocean and started tilting it up and down.

'Surf's up!' announced Woody.

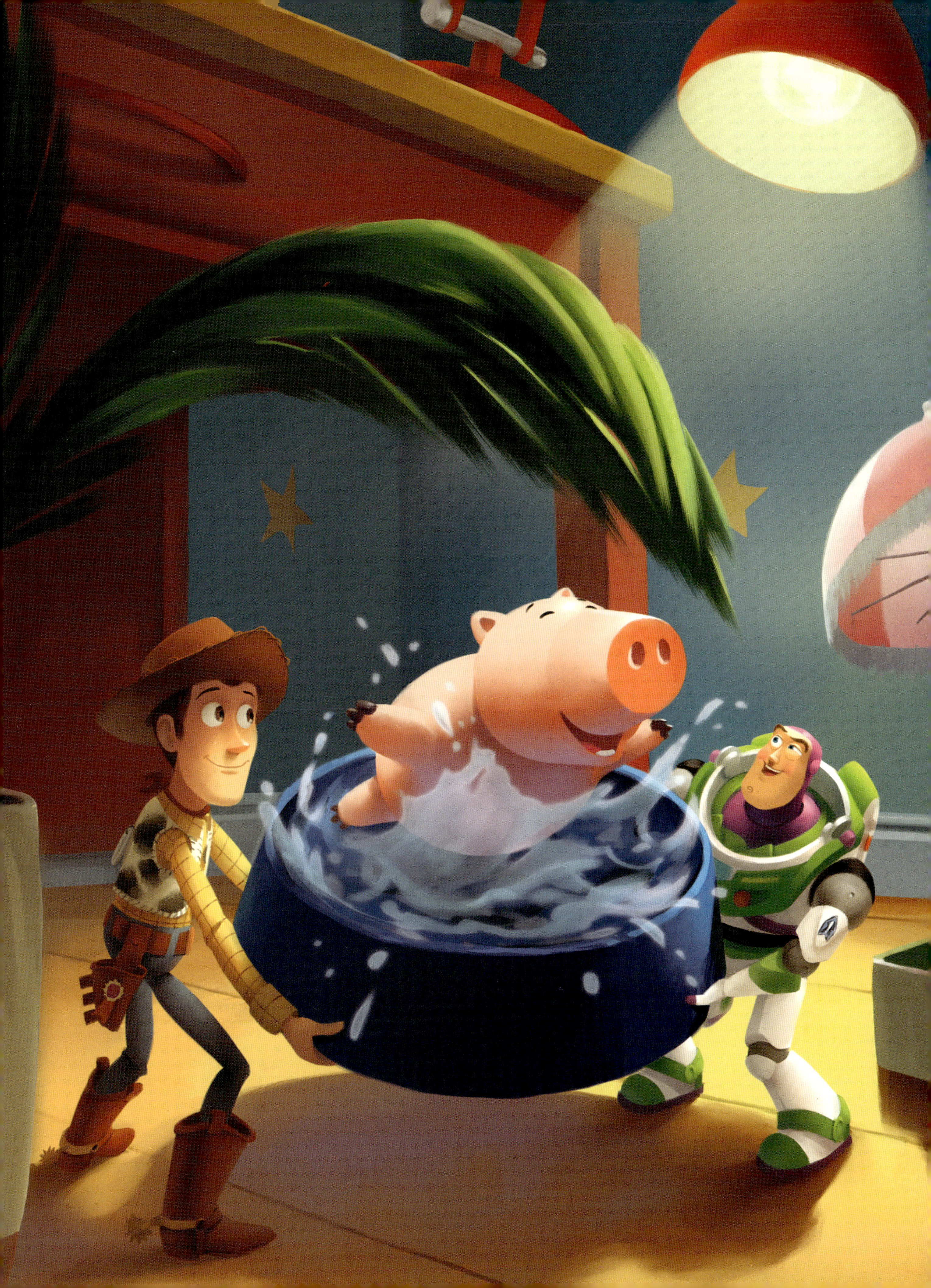

Jessie enjoyed a lively game of volleyball with Bullseye. Afterwards, she sat by the water and admired the view. Then she realised something was missing—an ocean breeze!

She got up and lassoed a knob on Andy's dresser. Once the rope was secure, she began to climb. When she made it to the top, she flipped a switch.

A slight breeze started.

'What's that?' Woody said.

Within seconds, the wind picked up, blowing things everywhere. The toys scurried for cover as the parasol and the beach chairs skittered across the room.

'Typhoon!' Rex cried, diving under the bed.

'It's okay!' Jessie called. She flipped off the switch and the wind stopped. 'It was just the fan. Is everyone okay?'

'Almost everyone,' Woody said. He pointed towards the bed where Rex's tail poked out from under the bedspread.

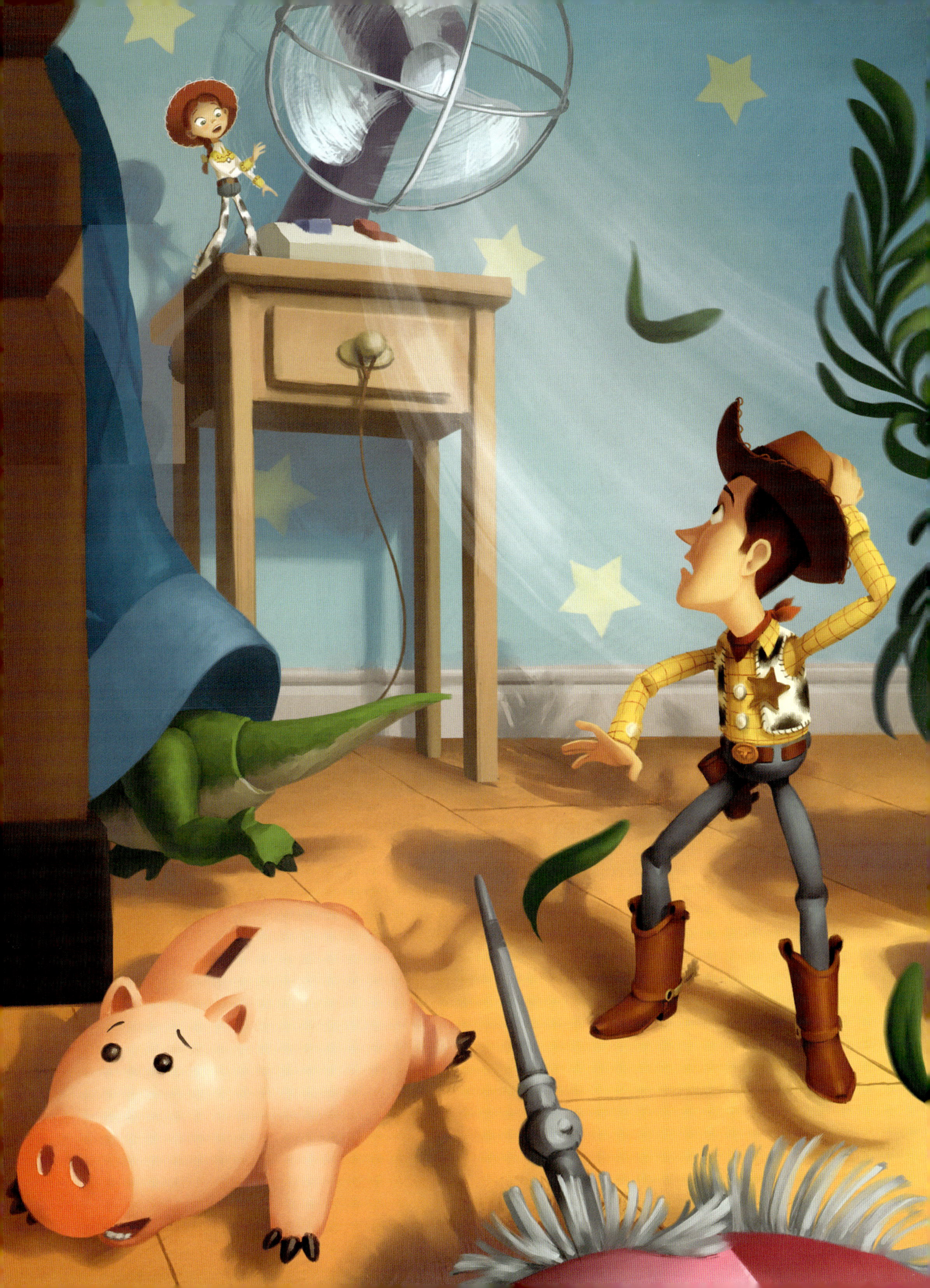

It took a little while, but finally, Jessie and the rest of the toys convinced Rex to come out of his hiding place. He was still trembling with fear.

'I don't think I can survive another relaxing holiday!' the dinosaur said.

'Don't worry, Rex,' Woody said. 'There won't be any more storms here today.'

'Woody's right,' Jessie chimed in. She put the parasol back in its place, shading the lounge chairs from the 'sun'. 'We're in for clear skies and warm weather.'

Rex walked back over to the beach. 'I hope Andy has a great trip,' he said. 'Because paradise can be fun . . . as long as you're with good friends.'

Toy Story 3

So Long, Partner

Over the years, Andy had had a lot of fun playing with his toys. He set up an old Western town in his bedroom and played battle the bandits with them. Sheriff Woody, the cowboy doll, always saved the day.

Andy used his Buzz Lightyear action figure to teach the other toys to 'fly'. He would swoop the space ranger around the backyard with Jessie the cowgirl and Bullseye the horse. Then he'd have the toys save the galaxy from Buzz's enemy, the evil Emperor Zurg!

At birthday parties or scary-movie nights, Andy would bring along his toys to join in the fun. Woody or Buzz went with him everywhere: to the park, to Pizza Planet or to a friend's house for a sleepover. And after a long day of fun and adventure, Andy would fall asleep next to his old pals and dream about all the games they would play the next day.

The years passed quickly and before the toys knew it, Andy was getting ready to go to college.

The toys had known this day was coming. But knowing didn't make them any less scared.

'No-one's getting thrown out,' Woody assured his friends. 'We're all still here! Through every garage sale, every spring cleaning, Andy held onto us.'

When Andy's mum came upstairs to help Andy pack, she said that anything not packed for college or put in a bag for the attic would be thrown out.

'No-one's going to want those old toys,' Andy said. He put Jessie, Rex, the Little Green Aliens and some other toys in a garbage bag to go up to the attic.

Then he picked up Woody and Buzz. He looked first at Buzz. Then at Woody. With a sigh, he put Woody in a box marked COLLEGE. Then he tossed Buzz into the bag.

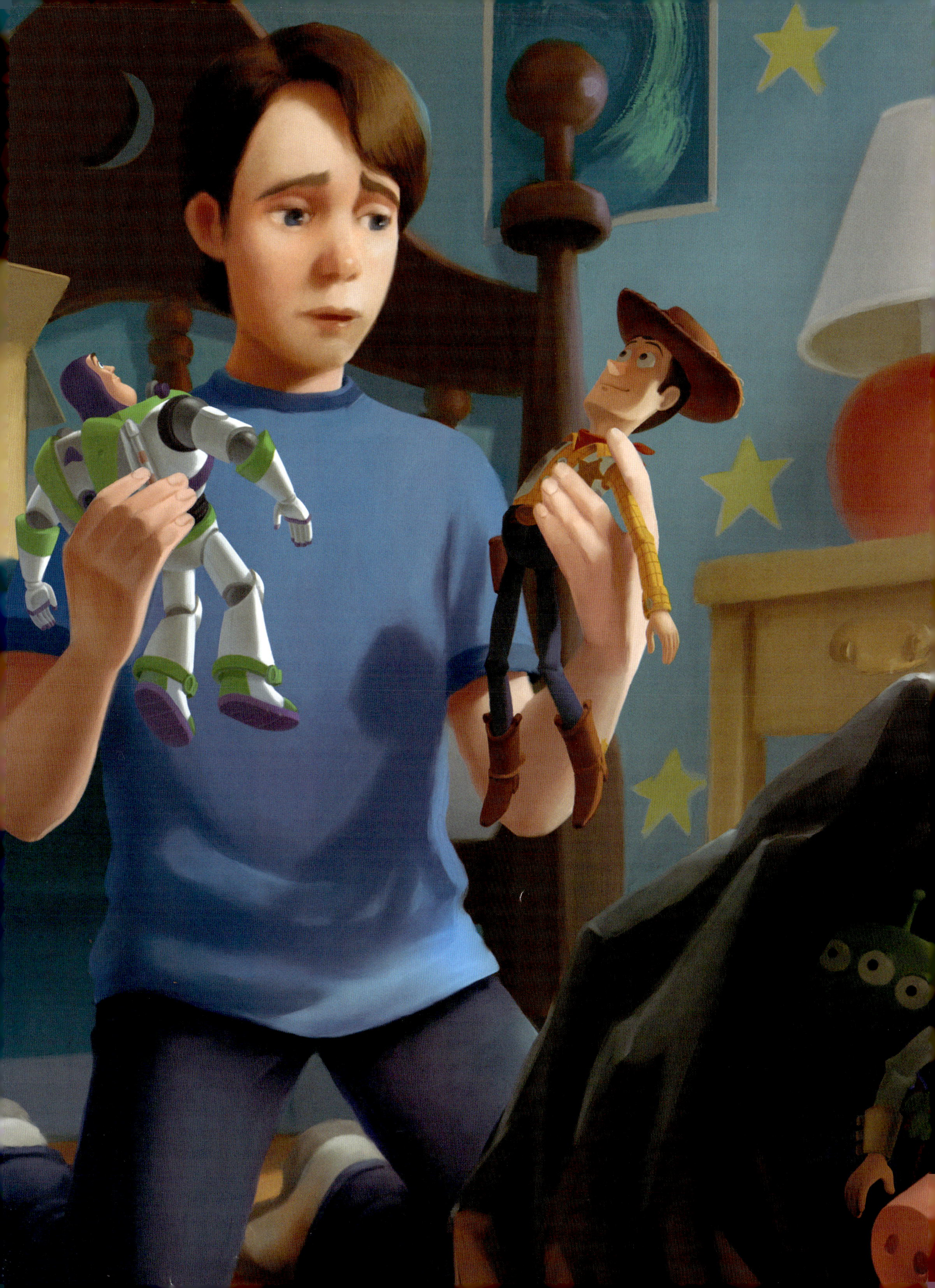

But Andy's mum threw out the trash bag with the toys inside by mistake.

Luckily, the toys escaped from the bag and ran into the garage. They climbed into a box in the back of the car. It was filled with some old toys that would be taken to a day care centre.

Buzz hesitated. 'What about Woody?'

'Andy's takin' him to college!' Jessie said. 'We need to go!'

Woody had followed his friends outside to rescue them. He tried to convince them that Andy wanted to put them in the attic. But the other toys wouldn't listen. They wanted to go to the day care centre to be played with. Woody went with them, hoping he could change their minds.

When the toys arrived at Sunnyside Daycare they saw kids playing everywhere. 'We hit the jackpot, Bullseye!' Jessie said.

'Well, hello there! Welcome to Sunnyside, folks!' said a pink plush teddy bear. 'Please, call me Lotso.'

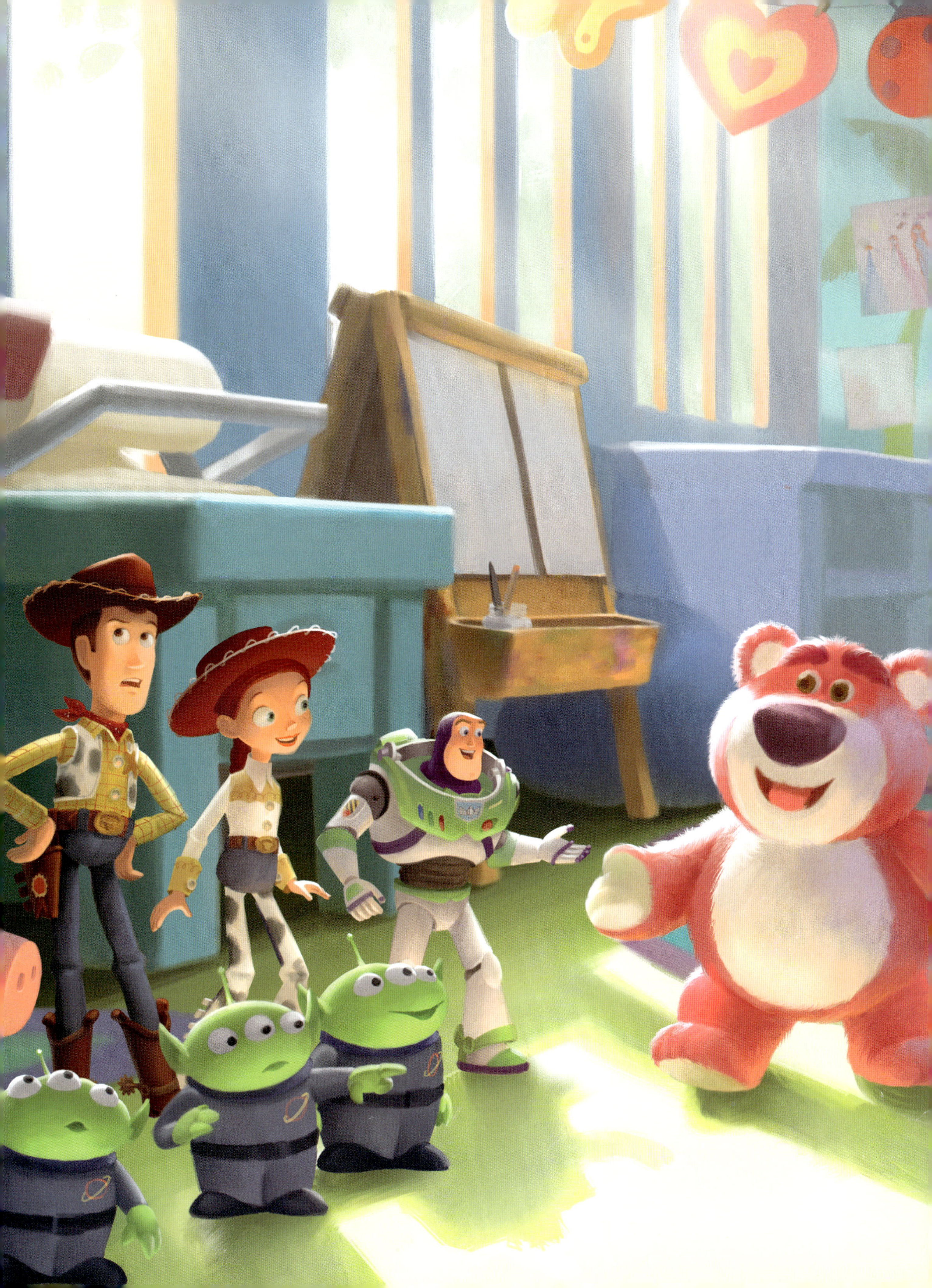

Lotso explained that at Sunnyside, toys were played with every day. There were always new kids to love them.

But Woody didn't want to make a new kid happy. 'You have a kid—Andy,' he reminded the others. 'If he wants us at college, or in the attic, well, then that's where we should be. Now, I'm going home. C'mon Buzz!'

Buzz didn't move. 'Our mission with Andy is complete, Woody.'

Jessie crossed her arms. 'Wake up! It's over. Andy is all grown up.'

The toys glanced sadly at one another.

'I gotta go,' Woody told his friends. Then he walked out.

The toys couldn't wait to be played with, but the children were much rougher than they were used to. Slinky was stretched to his limit. Rex's tail was snapped off. Jessie's hair was used as a paintbrush. Hamm was coated with glue and covered with macaroni and glitter. A little boy stuck Buzz's head in his mouth! It was awful.

Thunk! Buzz was tossed onto a windowsill. He peered through the window into another classroom. There, he saw Lotso and some of his friends, like Big Baby and Stretch the rubber octopus, being held gently by some older kids. The children quietly cuddled the toys as they listened to a story. Then someone picked up Buzz and threw him back into the chaos.

That night Buzz went to speak with Lotso about getting moved to the room with the big kids. When he found Lotso and his friends, Buzz overheard the toys talking about him and the rest of Andy's toys.

'All them toys are disposable,' said Twitch.

'Chuck' em,' Stretch added.

Buzz had to warn his friends! But Big Baby saw him.

'Stop! Let me go!' Buzz cried as Lotso's gang grabbed him. Seconds later he was tied to a chair. Lotso's gang pushed a button to reset Buzz's memory so he couldn't warn his friends.

Meanwhile, the rest of Andy's toys were recovering from a hard day. They started to think they'd made a terrible mistake by coming to the day care centre. Andy had always loved them, and taken good care of them. They realised that Woody had been right. They were Andy's toys! They didn't belong at Sunnyside.

Jessie hopped up. 'Guys—we gotta go home!'

But before they could move, Lotso and his gang came in with Buzz. They herded Andy's toys into storage baskets. Lotso didn't want Andy's toys to leave. In the day care centre, the new toys were for the little kids to play roughly with. Lotso and his friends didn't want to get dipped in paint and pulled apart!

Jessie looked at Buzz. He would save them!

Except Buzz didn't even seem to know his old friends. He tackled Rex and then knocked down the other toys.

'Prisoners, disabled, Commander Lotso!' he said.

Andy's toys looked at each other. What had happened to Buzz?

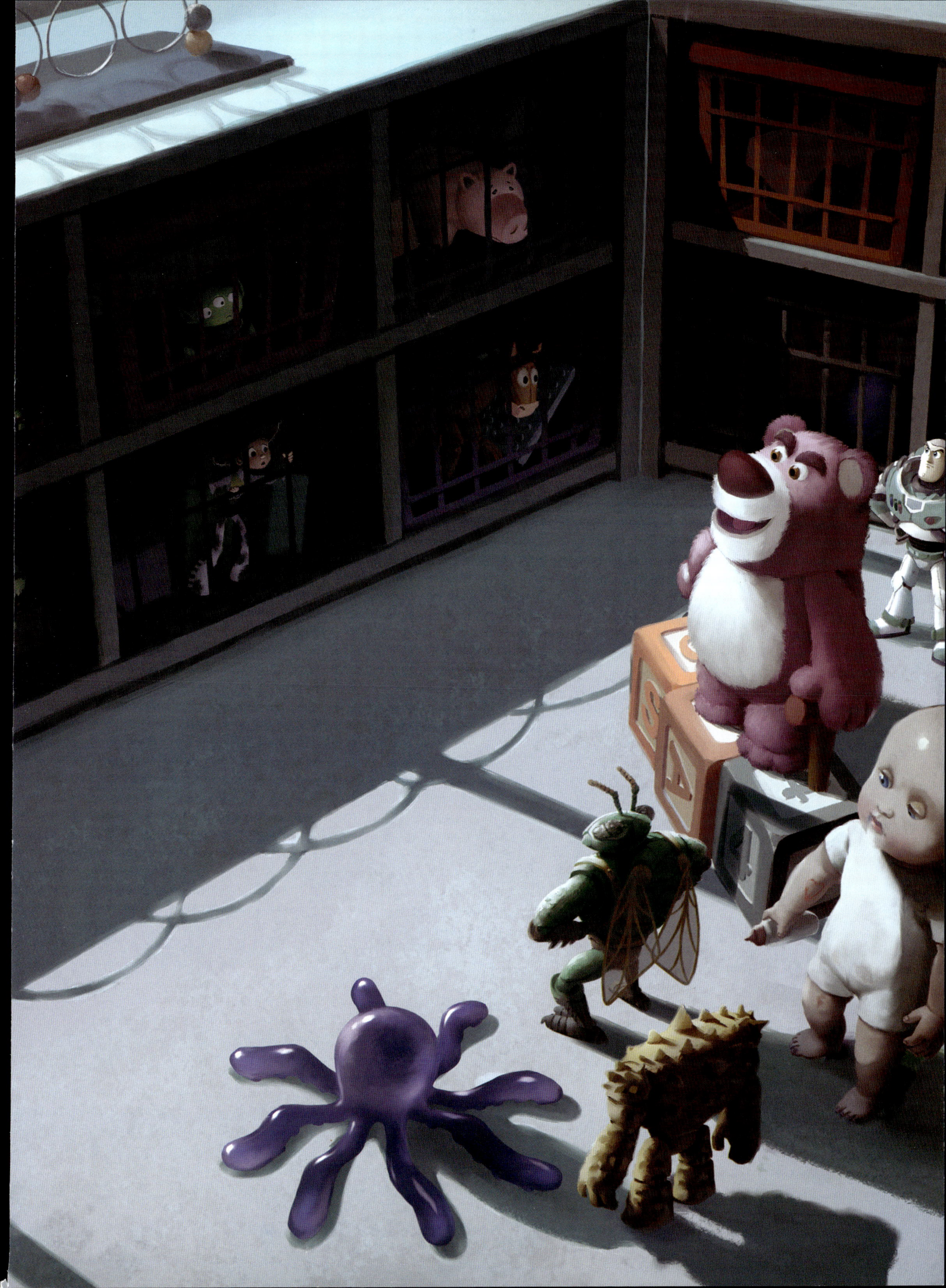

After Woody had left Sunnyside, he'd been taken home by a little girl named Bonnie. Her toys knew all about Lotso. They told Woody that Lotso had once belonged to a girl named Daisy. Daisy accidentally left Lotso at a rest stop. Lotso never forgave her for leaving him behind.

Woody hid in Bonnie's backpack so he could get back to the day care centre. He had to save his friends!

When Woody got to Sunnyside, his friends told him everything that had happened.

'From now on, we stick together. We're busting out of here tonight,' Woody said. Then he told them his plan.

First, they found Buzz. Woody pushed another button and Buzz started speaking Spanish. But he was on their side again! Then, they snuck outside.

Big Baby was on the swing. The toys crept across the playground behind him, heading for the garbage chute.

But Lotso was waiting for them. 'What are you all doing? Running back to your kid?' Lotso asked. 'He doesn't want you!'

Soon, Lotso ended up in the garbage bin. He tried to pull Woody in after him. When Andy's toys went to help Woody, they all tumbled in.

Before they could climb out of the garbage bin, the garbage truck came to pick it up. After a bumpy ride, Buzz snapped back to his old self. But the toys were dumped onto a moving conveyor belt headed for the shredder!

Jessie spotted a magnetic belt. The toys began grabbing metal objects that lifted them onto the magnetic belt. But then they were trapped on a new belt, headed towards a fire. Lotso appeared in front of the emergency stop button.

'Push it!' Woody yelled. But Lotso just laughed and ran away.

'Buzz, what do we do?' Jessie asked. Buzz took her hand. The toys closed their eyes as they got closer to the fire.

A shadow passed over Woody's face. He opened his eyes. A giant claw was lowering itself over the toys' heads. The jaws opened and picked everyone up.

'The Claw!' squeaked the Aliens as they manned the controls. They had seen the claw as soon as they landed in the garbage. They always knew it would help them get home!

At last, the toys made it back to Andy's. Everyone climbed into the ATTIC box as Woody and Buzz said goodbye.

Then Woody had an idea. He stuck a note on the box with Bonnie's address.

Andy took the box to Bonnie's house. 'These are my toys,' he told Bonnie. 'I need someone really special to play with them.'

He showed Bonnie each toy. Then he came to Woody. 'What's he doing in here? He's been my pal for as long as I can remember.' Andy smiled. Giving Woody one last squeeze, Andy handed Woody to Bonnie. Then, he got in his car.

Bonnie went inside with her mother. The toys sat together, watching Andy drive away. 'So long, partner,' Woody said.

Buzz put his arm around Woody's shoulders. Even though they didn't have Andy, they knew everything would be just fine. After all, they had each other. And a new kid who'd love them the way Andy had.

THE END